INSURANCE LEARNERS

AVIATION LAW AND CLAIMS

by

M.J. Spurway

LONDON
WITHERBY & CO. LTD.
32-36 Aylesbury Street
London EC1R OET
Tel No. 071-251 5341
Fax No. 071-251 1296

1st Edition 1992

©

WITHERBY & CO. LTD.
1992
ISBN 1 85609 031 0

Printed in Great Britain by
Witherby & Co. Ltd.
London

CONTENTS

INTRODUCTION

The "Insurance Learners" Series was first published by Lesley and Page Services Limited over 10 years ago. Some titles are now in their fourth or fifth edition. Learners are aimed at all readers who wish to have a basic grounding in the various aspects of insurance covered by each title. In particular they are invaluable, low cost introductory and revision texts for the qualifying examinations of the:—

Chartered Insurance Institute (CII) and BTEC

They are also useful additional reading on insurance aspects of other professional examinations and further and higher education courses, and are used extensively within the training departments of insurance organisations.

Most of the Learners include examples of past examination questions and examiners' comments from the Chartered Insurance Institute.

With the introduction of the new CII examination syllabus in 1992, some titles in the series are being extensively revised. For these titles past examination questions are not included, although they will be in future editions. Students using the 'Learners' to help with their examinations should check the current syllabus carefully and revise those parts from the 'Learner' which are most relevant. For CII students, the Publishers, Witherby & Company have an up to date list of which titles are most useful for each of the CII examination subjects.

The Learners are not a substitute for the full recommended texts of the examining body concerned, especially the CII. Neither are they an examination "crammer". Rather, they are designed to be used as introductory reading, to get an overview of the subject. Also most importantly, they are an invaluable revision aid, providing a succinct summary of each topic area covered in order to fix the subject in the mind and refresh the memory.

As always, the Publishers and the Authors welcome any comments from readers and would like to thank those who have, in the past, made useful suggestions incorporated in current editions.

730 — AVIATION LAW AND CLAIMS

KNOWLEDGE BASE

The Development of Aviation Law

- Historical developments giving rise to the Warsaw Convention 1929 including
  - the scope and language of the Convention
  - ticketing requirements
  - baggage and cargo liability.
- The further development of air carrier legislation (and variations from country to country) with regard to aircraft operators and manufacturers including
  - the Hague Protocol 1955 and how this updated the Warsaw Convention
  - the Montreal Agreement 1966
  - the Guatemala Protocol 1971 and current thinking on the possible application of its provisions
  - the Guadalajara Convention 1961
  - the Carriage by Air Act 1961 and subsequent UK legislation
  - an outline knowledge of other international conventions governing passenger and third party liability.

Operational Considerations

- An outline knowledge of legislation affecting the operation and licensing of aircraft and aircrews including
  - in the UK the ARB and CAA
  - in the USA the FAA and NTSB
  - internationally the ICAO.

The USA

- The basic structure of the legal system in the USA including
  - the different jurisdictions
  - compulsory insurance requirements
  - litigation procedure
  - punitive damages and the position of insurers.

Claims

- The methods of investigation and handling of hull and liability claims within the boundaries of the various legislative systems and taking account of the various international conventions relating to carriage by air including
  - liaison with legal representatives
  - the prosecution of subrogation claims
  - an outline knowledge of court procedures, out of court settlements and *ex gratia* payments.
- The role of the aviation claims adjuster in the handling and settlement of claims including
  - claims procedures within the London aviation market (special settlements, letters of credit, sharing agreements)
  - claims handling on reinsurance contracts, claims control and co-operation clauses
  - familiarity with relevant legislation worldwide.

NOTE TO CANDIDATES

Candidates will be required to
- compare and evaluate the various liability regimes in force and identify the effect these have on settlement of claims
- explain the methods of defence and prosecution of claims against aircraft and component manufacturers and offer opinions on effecting claims reporting and reserving practices.

ABOUT THE AUTHOR

John Spurway has been involved in the insurance industry for thirty years and specialises in the technical aspects of Aviation Insurance.

He joined J.K. Seear and Company Ltd., Lloyd's Brokers in 1961. The company enlarged and expanded over the years to become Cayzer, Steel, Bowater International Ltd., of which he became a Director. He is presently a Director of the Insurance Brokers Division of Morgan, Read and Sharman Ltd., Lloyd's Brokers. He has been registered with the Insurance Brokers Registration Council since 1982.

CHAPTER 1

THE WARSAW CONVENTION (1929)

1.1 HISTORICAL DEVELOPMENT

The French convened the first international conference on air law in Paris in 1889 as a result of the development of the balloon (which by then had proved its ability to cross the channel). The implications of a vehicle that could cross international boundaries without hindrance and yet potentially cause damage on the ground was not lost on either governments or the legal profession. The first conference at The Hague in 1899 declared that the discharge of projectiles from balloons 'or other new methods of a similar nature' be prohibited. At the second Hague conference in 1907 many of the nations previously represented refused however to renew that resolution as the true aeroplane had by then flown. In 1909, the year of Bleriot's epoch making flight across the channel, an independent group of international lawyers meeting in Paris founded the International Committee of Aviation Law to discuss the rules of public international law and the conflicting laws of different countries. In 1910 the representatives of 19 nations met in Paris but could not agree upon an international code of air law. Such meetings were suspended during the World War I period, 1914-18, though in 1916 the Pan-American Aeronautical Conference met in Chile and recommended that all the American Republics should have uniform aviation legislation with a view to forming an international air code, which was not in the end adopted.

1.2 CONVENTION OF PARIS

In 1919 the Powers assembled in Paris for the Peace Conference discussed and agreed rules for the regulation of international aviation. These were put into the form of an international convention, signed on 13th October 1919 and became known as the Convention of Paris. (A convention is a provisional treaty between sovereign states but does not bind those states unless and until it is ratified by them. Non-signatories may 'adhere' to the convention). This particular Convention established rules governing flight over and between different states as well as affirming the complete and exclusive sovereignty of every state over the airspace above its territory − a subject re-opened with our entry to the space age, to the extent that upper air sovereignty arguably should be set at less than the height at which it is possible to place a satellite in orbit. The Convention also laid down rules governing the fitness of aircraft and their crew, and others governing navigation. It was signed by 38 countries but not the majority of the American Republics (including the USA) so the aim of universal agreement failed. Great Britain, a signatory, ratified the Convention by the Air Navigation Act 1920 subsequently superceeded by the Civil Aviation Act 1949 (as was the 1919 Paris Convention superseded by the Chicago Convention 1944). In 1928 the Pan American Convention was signed in Havana.

1.3 INTERNATIONAL CONFLICT OF LAW

By this time, although air transport itself was flourishing its regulation was a muddle. Different legal systems approached problems in different ways. The rights of passengers and cargo owners and liabilities of the operators depended on legislation developed for land and sea transit. Not only was there uncertainty as to the content of applicable law but in international carriage there were choice of law problems in the conflict of laws.

The International Air Traffic Association, founded in 1919, the precursor of IATA, had produced specimen uniform conditions of carriage but even when these were used it was back to the courts as to how they would be interpreted.

1.4 THE BIRTH OF THE WARSAW CONVENTION

In 1925 at the first session of the Conference Internationale de Droit Privé Aérien (CIDPA), held in Paris, a specialist committee was established – Comité International Technique d'Experts Juridiques Aeriens (CITEJA) – whose brief was to put an end to the conflicts of law problems inherent in international carriage by air. As a result of their deliberations in October 1929 at CIDPA's second meeting held in Warsaw, a convention 'for the unification of certain rules relating to international Carriage by Air' was produced. It was signed on the 12th October 1929 on behalf of 23 countries. It came into effect 90 days after the deposit with the Government of Poland of the 5th instrument of ratification. It has since been ratified by most countries of the world.

There exist the working notes leading to the final Convention wording, known as the traveux préparatoires, rarely used, but they exist and have been used (for example, Fothergill v. Monarch Airlines Ltd. House of Lords 1981) to interpret intent and the object and purpose of the provision that might be in question.

The Warsaw Convention itself sought to solve the problems arising from conflict of laws arising from international flying. It set a precedent for the modern concept of no-fault liability. Provided the proper form of words had been used in the passenger ticket or contract of carriage, negligence on the part of the airline did not have to be proved. In return a limitation was placed on the carriers liability and the plaintiff only had to prove quantum of his damage.

The Warsaw Convention was written in a single official language, French, being that of diplomacy of the day. (A single copy was deposited in the archives of the Ministry of Foreign Affairs of Poland and only one duly certified copy was to be sent by the Polish Government to each signatory of the Convention). It was given legal effect in English law by the Carriage by Air Act 1932, which Act has since been repealed under provision contained in the Carriage by Air Act 1961, which introduced the amendments contained in the Hague Protocol of 1955, though the 1961 Act did not come into force until the passing by the UK Parliament of the Carriage by Air Acts (Application of Provisions) Order 1967.

1.5 SUMMARY OF THE WARSAW CONVENTION

The Convention applies to **contracts** for **international** carriage only – the place of departure and the place of destination are the only factors that matter; nationality of carrier or passenger are irrelevant. International is defined as carriage which according to the contract between the parties, has the place of departure within the territory of one High Contracting State and the place of destination in that of another, or both destination and departure are within the territory of a single High Contracting State **but** with an agreed stopping place within the territory of another power whether or not that power is a signatory to the Convention (Article 1). It applies equally to carriage performed for reward and to gratuitous carriage by an air transport undertaking (Article 1). It applies also to carriage performed by the State or a public body (Article 2). In all cases a ticket or 'Airwaybill' must be issued in an approved format. It should be noted that although the term 'air transport undertaking' used above is taken from the Convention it is not defined therein. The Convention does not apply to carriage performed under the terms of any international postal convention (Article 2), nor to internal flights within a single state or territory, nor unusual carriage or route proving flights/trial flights.

A carriage to be performed by several successive air carriers is deemed for the purposes of the Convention to be one undivided carriage **provided** it has been regarded by the parties as a single operation whether under the form of a single contract or series of contracts. To decide whether it is international or not the **entire operation** must be considered; it does not lose its international character merely because one contract or a series of contracts are not international (Article 1).

In the case of carriage performed by successive carriers each carrier who accepts passengers, luggage or goods is subject to the rules of the Convention and is deemed to be one of the contracting parties to the Contract of carriage in so far as that part of the carriage is concerned which is performed under his supervision (Article 30).

In the case of carriage of this nature, the passenger or his representative can take action only against the carrier who performed the carriage during which the accident or the delay occurred, save in the case where, by express agreement, the first carrier has assumed liability for the whole journey.

As regards luggage or goods, the passenger or consignor will have a right of action against the first carrier, and the passenger or consignee who is entitled to delivery will have a right of action against the last carrier, and further, each may take action against the carrier who performed the carriage during which the destruction, loss, damage, or delay took place. These carriers will be jointly and severally liable to the passenger or to the consignor or consignee (Article 30).

Note   – to be 'successive carriage'

(a)   the passenger and the first carrier must regard the whole journey as a single operation.

(b)   the journey must be clearly divided into separate stages.

(c)   the parties must have agreed at the outset to the employment of successive carriers.

(the question of substitution of a carrier during the journey, by either the carrier or the passenger, invoking the contractual right to do so in the Contract of Carriage has never yet been satisfactorily resolved).

1.5.1   The Passenger Ticket

Before making a flight a passenger agrees with the carrier the journey to be undertaken, the fare is paid, a ticket issued and the contract thereby bound. The ticket now becomes paramount. To obtain the protection of the Convention the carrier must deliver the passenger his ticket a sufficient time before the flight to enable him to make other arrangements if the conditions contained in it do not suit him. It is not good enough to hand the ticket over on board the aircraft or just before boarding (see Warren v Flying Tiger Line 1965 and/or Martens v Flying Tiger Line 1965, both US cases) and the print size on the ticket referring to the limitation of the carriers liability under the Convention must be of a size and location so as to be easily readable for the same reasons (see Lisi v Alitalia 1966 and Egam v Kollsman Instrument Corp. 1967 – again both US cases). The ticket must contain the following particulars:

(a)   the place and date of issue;

(b)   the place of departure and of destination;

(c)   the agreed stopping places, provided that the carrier may reserve the right to alter the stopping places in case of necessity, and that if he exercises that right, the alteration shall not have the effect of depriving the carriage of its international character;

(d)   the name and address of the carrier or carriers;

(e)   a statement that the carriage is subject to the rules relating to liability established by this Convention (Article 3)

The absence, irregularity or loss of the passenger ticket does not affect the existence or the validity of the contract of carriage, which shall none the less be subject to the rules of the Convention. Nevertheless, if the carrier accepts a passenger without a passenger ticket having been delivered he shall not be entitled to avail himself of those provisions of the Convention which exclude or limit his liability (Article 3).

As previously mentioned, carriage may be performed by several successive carriers but the ticket still governs the situation. Breaks in the carriage do not count, so a return ticket for a holiday abroad counts as one contract even with the gap of a holiday between the flight out and the flight back and because the landing outside the country of departure counts as international. A flight out and back, no matter how far it goes (for example, Concorde day trips) which does not land outside the country of departure is not international. There must be a planned landing outside the country of departure (see UK case, Grein v Imperial Airways 1937).

1.5.2 The Luggage (Baggage) Ticket
(Usually – per Hague Protocol – now built in to the passenger ticket and not issued separately).

For the carriage of luggage, other than small personal objects of which the passenger takes charge himself, the carrier must deliver a luggage ticket.

The luggage ticket shall be made out in duplicate, one part for the passenger and the other part for the carrier.

The luggage ticket shall contain the following particulars:

(a)   the place and date of issue;

(b)   the place of departure and of destination;

(c)   the name and address of the carrier or carriers;

(d)   the number of the passenger ticket;

(e)   a statement that delivery of the luggage will be made to the bearer of the luggage ticket;

(f)   the number and weight of the packages;

(g)   the amount of the value declared in accordance with Article 22 (2) ;

(h)   a statement that the carriage is subject to the rules relating to liability established by this Convention.

The absence, irregularity or loss of the luggage ticket does not affect the existence or the validity of the contract of carriage, which shall none the less be subject to the rules of the Convention. Nevertheless, if the carrier accepts luggage without a luggage ticket having been delivered, or if the luggage ticket does not contain the particulars set out at (d), (f) and (h) above, the carrier shall not be entitled to avail himself of those provisions of the Convention which exclude or limit his liability (Article 4).

1.5.3 The Cargo (Freight) 'Ticket'
(Air Consignment Note)

Unlike the other two tickets which are issued by the carrier, this one is issued by the consignor. It is made out in three parts and handed over with the goods, part one is for the carrier and signed by the consignor, part two is for the consignee and accompanies the goods being signed by both consignor and carrier; part three is signed by the carrier and is given by him to the consignor on acceptance of the goods.

The consignor is responsible for the correctness of the particulars and statements relating to the goods which he inserts in the air consignment note, and is liable for all damage suffered by the carrier or any other person by reason of the irregularity, incorrectness or incompleteness of the said particulars and statements (Article 10).

The consignment note must contain the following particulars:

(a) the place and date of its execution;

(b) the place of departure and of destination;

(c) the agreed stopping places, provided that the carrier may reserve the right to alter the stopping places in case of necessity, and that if he exercises that right the alteration shall not have the effect of depriving the carriage of its international character;

(d) the name and address of the consignor;

(e) the name and address of the first carrier;

(f) the name and address of the consignee, if the case so requires;

(g) the nature of the goods;

(h) the number of the packages, the method of packing and the particular marks or numbers upon them;

(i) the weight, the quantity and the volume or dimensions of the goods;

(j) the apparent condition of the goods and of the packing;

(k) the freight, if it has been agreed upon, the date and place of payment, and the person who is to pay it;

(l) if the goods are sent for payment on delivery, the price of the goods, and, if the case so requires, the amount of the expenses incurred;

(m) the amount of the value declared in accordance with Article 22(2);

(n) the number of parts of the air consignment note;

(o) the documents handed to the carrier to accompany the air consignment note;

(p) the time fixed for the completion of the carriage and a brief note of the route to be followed, if these matters have been agreed upon;

(q)   a statement that the carriage is subject to the rules relating to liability established by this Convention.

If, at the request of the consignor, the carrier makes out the air consignment note, he shall be deemed, subject to proof to the contrary, to have done so on behalf of the consignor. (Article 8)

But note – omission of certain details do not necessarily invalidate the Convention requirements, e.g. the case Corocraft v Pan American World Airways inc. 1969; the air consignment note for a package of jewellery gave weight but omitted details of the specific content, volume and dimensions of the package. The Court of Appeal held weight must be given if appropriate (and it usually is) but the other conditions only if useful or necessary. In this case they were held not to be. (It cannot necessarily make good sense to label small packages 'extremely valuable jewellery' or 'diamonds').

The carrier of goods has the right to require the consignor to make out separate consignment notes when there is more than one package. (Article 7).

Every carrier of goods has the right to require the consignor to make out and hand over to him an 'air consignment note'; every consignor has the right to require the carrier to accept this document.

The absence, irregularity or loss of this document does not affect the existence or the validity of the contract of carriage which shall none the less be governed by the rules of the Convention. (Article 5).

If the carrier accepts goods without an air consignment note having been made out, or if the air consignment note does not contain all the particulars set out above, the carrier shall not be entitled to avail himself of the provisions of the Convention which exclude or limit his liability. (Article 9).

1.5.4 The Liability of the Carrier
The carrier is liable for damage sustained in the event of the death or wounding of a passenger or any other bodily injury suffered by a passenger, if the accident which caused the damage so sustained took place on board the aircraft or in the course of any of the operations of embarking or disembarking (Article 17).

The carrier is liable for damage sustained in the event of the destruction or loss of, or of damage to, any registered luggage or any goods, if the occurrence which caused the damage so sustained took place during the carriage by air. The carriage by air comprises the period during which the luggage or goods are in charge of the carrier, whether in an aerodrome or on board an aircraft, or, in the case of a landing outside an aerodrome, in any place whatsoever.

The period of the carriage by air does not extend to any carriage by land, by sea or by river performed outside an aerodrome. If, however, such a carriage takes place in the performance of a contract for carriage by air, for the purpose of loading, delivery or trans-shipment, any damage is presumed, subject to proof to the contrary, to have been the result of an event which took place during the carriage by air (Article 18).

The carrier is liable for damage occasioned by delay in the carriage by air of passengers, luggage or goods (Article 19).

In the carriage of passengers the liability of the carrier for each passenger is limited to the sum of 125,000 francs. Nevertheless, by special contract, the carrier and the passenger may agree to a higher limit of liability.

In the carriage of registered luggage and of goods, the liability of the carrier is limited to a sum of 250 francs per kilogram, unless the consignor has made, at the time when the package was handed over to the carrier, a special declaration of the value at delivery and has paid a supplementary sum if the case so requires. In that case the carrier will be liable to pay a sum not exceeding the declared sum, unless he proves that the sum is greater than the actual value to the consignor at delivery.

As regards objects of which the passenger takes charge himself the liability of the carrier is limited to 5,000 francs per passenger.

The sums mentioned above shall be deemed to refer to the French franc consisting of 65 1/2 milligrams gold of millesimal fineness 900. These sums may be converted into any national currency in round figures (Article 22).

Any condition that the carrier introduced into the contract of carriage to relieve himself of liability or fix a lower limit of liability than those shown above is null and void (Article 23).

The carrier is only liable if any action for damages, however founded, is brought subject to the conditions and limits of the Convention. In the case of passengers (as opposed to goods) this is without prejudice as to who are the persons who have the right to bring suit and what are their respective rights (Article 24).

The carrier shall not be entitled to avail himself of the provisions of the Convention which exclude or limit his liability, if the damage is caused by his wilful misconduct (or that of any agent of his acting within the scope of his employment) or by such default on his (or their) part as, in accordance with the law of the Court seized of the case, is considered to be equivalent to wilful misconduct (Article 25).

Note the words 'wilful misconduct' above. This is the closest approximation of the French word 'dol' (it will be recalled this Convention has only one official text – French). This has led to problems in the Courts from time to time, hence all subsequent amendments to the Convention have had official texts in at least three 'official' languages, one of which has been English.

1.5.5 The Carrier's Defences

The carrier is not liable if he proves that he and his agents have taken all necessary measures to avoid the damage or that it was impossible for him or them to take such measures.

In the carriage of goods and luggage the carrier is not liable if he proves that the damage was occasioned by negligent pilotage or negligence in the handling of the aircraft or in navigation and that, in all other respects, he and his agents have taken all necessary measures to avoid the damage (Article 20 – but note however this will not prove a defence where injury to a passenger is concerned). If the carrier proves that the damage was caused by or contributed to by the negligence of the injured person the Court may, in accordance with the provisions of its own law, exonerate the carrier wholly or partly from his liability (Article 21).

The right to damages shall be extinguished if an action is not brought within two years from the date of arrival at the destination, or from the date on which the aircraft ought to have arrived, or from the date on which the carriage stopped (Article 29).

It should be noted that in stipulating that the liability of the carrier to passengers devolves only during embarkation, whilst on board the aircraft and whilst disembarking, at any other time he has no liability under the Convention, but he might well have under common law and civil law.

Receipt by the person entitled to delivery of luggage or goods without complaint is prima facie evidence that the same have been delivered in good condition and in accordance with the document of carriage.

In the case of damage, the person entitled to delivery must complain to the carrier forthwith after the discovery of the damage, and, at the latest, within three days from the date of receipt in the case of luggage and seven days from the date of receipt in the case of goods. In the case of delay the complaint must be made at the latest within fourteen days from the date on which the luggage or goods have been placed at his disposal.

Every complaint must be made in writing upon the document of carriage or by separate notice in writing despatched within the times aforesaid.

Failing complaint within the times aforesaid, no action shall lie against the carrier, save in the case of fraud on his part (Article 26).

1.5.6 General Conditions

The Convention permits the carrier to reserve his right to change the agreed stopping places if the need arises without altering the contractual position.

The carriers employees working as flight, deck or cabin crew on an aircraft are not passengers and the limits of the Convention would not apply to them, neither indeed would Section 3 of AVN 1A and protection against liability to them would have to be sought in Employers Liability/Workmen's Compensation Act insurance.

An employees position as regards their liability under the Convention if they themselves are sued is not made clear by that document so it is usual for the carrier to insert the necessary protective wording into the Contract with the passenger.

In the case of the death of the person liable, an action for damages lies in accordance with the terms of the Convention against those legally representing his estate (Article 27). An action for damages must be brought, at the option of the plaintiff, in the territory of one of the High Contracting Parties, either before the Court having jurisdiction where the carrier is ordinarily resident, or has his principal place of business, or has an establishment by which the contract has been made or before the Court having jurisdiction at the place of destination.

Questions of procedure shall be governed by the law of the Court seized of the case.

Nothing contained in the Convention shall prevent the carrier either from refusing to enter into any contract of carriage, or from making regulations which do not conflict with the provisions of this Convention (Article 33).

In the case of combined carriage performed partly by air and partly by any other mode of carriage, the provisions of this Convention apply only to the carriage by air. But it should be noted that this would include immediately related land carriage such as by bus from the terminal to the aircraft. Nothing in the Convention shall prevent the parties in the case of combined carriage from inserting in the document of air carriage conditions relating to other modes of carriage, provided that the provisions of the Convention are observed as regards the carriage by air (Article 31).

The use of another means of transport between two flights does not affect the position of the air carrier either side of the other means of transport, provided it naturally forms part of the whole journey (see US case Egan v Kollsman Instrument Corp.)

The gold franc referred to under the heading 'The Liability of the Carrier' is known as the Poincaré franc after the French finance minister at the time. The reason for the use of gold was, as M. Pittard, the Swiss delegate said in the minutes of the Warsaw Convention, to avoid using a specific national currency which could possibly be at any time devalued. Gold was, and is readily convertible into any currency and provides a stable (and indeed, within limits) an inflation proof level of benefit.

Provision was made to enable any High Contracting Party to call upon the Government of France to convene an international conference to consider any improvements that might be made to the Convention (Article 41).

CHAPTER 2

THE FURTHER DEVELOPMENT OF AIR CARRIER LEGISLATION
(AND NATIONAL VARIATIONS)

2.1   THE HAGUE PROTOCOL

The Warsaw Convention had been seen to stand the test of time but there were certain aspects that created pressure for change from the international community, particularly the USA, and eventually, in 1955, a meeting was arranged at The Hague to remedy these shortcomings and to bring the Convention up to date. As a result the Hague Protocol was promulgated making the following changes to the underlying Warsaw Convention:

In the definition of International Carriage the High Contracting Parties must be signatories to the Hague Protocol. Signing of the Protocol by a state not a party to the Warsaw Convention has the effect of signing at the same time the Warsaw Convention.

Carriage is not international except as understood by the amended Convention.

The amended Convention does not apply to carriage performed for military or other authorities of a state.

Carriage of mail and postal packets remain excepted.

It will be recalled that in Article 25 of the Convention translation of the French word 'dol' had given difficulty. In Article 13 of the Protocol the problem paragraphs were re-phrased so that the limits of liability should not apply if proved that the damage resulted from an act or omission of the carrier, his servants or agents done with intent to cause damage or recklessly and with knowledge that damage would probably result, provided that in the case of such act of omission of a servant or agent, it is also proved that he was acting within the scope of his employment.

Servants or agents are given the protection of the amended Convention provided they can prove that they acted within the scope of their employment.

2.1.1   Limitation and Liability

Passengers – Limit doubled to 250,000 gold francs.
Baggage, Personal Baggage, and Goods (Cargo)
  – No changes from the Convention itself.

Additionally the Court may award Court costs and other expenses of the litigation incurred by the plaintiff **but** not if the amount of damages awarded excluding such costs and expenses does not exceed the sum which the carrier has offered in writing within six months from the date of the occurrence or before the date of the action.

Time limits for damage complaints were also amended from seven to fourteen days from receipt of cargo and from three to seven days for baggage. In the case of delay the time limit was extended from fourteen to twenty one days.

2.1.2   Passenger Tickets

A ticket must still be delivered but need now only contain the following:

(a)   an indication of the places of departure and destination.

(b)   if the above places are within the territory of a single state at least one stopping place within the territory of another state − if the journey is to be considered international.

(c)   (and mandatory). A notice to the effect that if the journey involves an ultimate destination or stop in a country other than the country of departure, the Warsaw Convention may be applicable and that the Convention governs and in most cases limits the liability of carriers for death or personal injury and in respect of loss of or damage to baggage.

(Without this notice being contained in the ticket in suitable print the carrier cannot limit his liability).

The ticket constitutes prima facie evidence of the conclusion and conditions of the contract; failure of delivery invalidates the carriers ability to limit his liability.

2.1.3 Baggage Ticket
This may now be combined with the passenger ticket and need now only contain the same information as required by the Hague Protocol for that ticket − as shown above. The comment relative to the 'Notice' and failure to deliver apply as for the passenger ticket.

2.1.4 Cargo Documentation
Again the requirement is for less information to appear and that needed is the same as for the passenger ticket except that reference to death or personal injury is deleted and the word baggage amended to cargo.

If with the consent of the carrier cargo is loaded on board the aircraft without an Airwaybill having been made out (and signed prior to such loading) or if the 'Notice' is not contained therein the carriers ability to limit his liability is invalidated.

The protocol also adds a new defence for the carrier in that he will not be liable for loss or damage resulting from the inherent defect, quality or vice of the cargo carried.

2.1.5 Carriers Defence
The defence under paragraph (2) of Article 20 of Warsaw regarding negligent pilotage, negligence in handling of the aircraft or in navigation is deleted in full.

2.1.6 Language
The Protocol was drafted in French, Spanish and English. It was brought into UK Law by the Carriage by Air Act 1961. The Protocol came into force 90 days after the thirtieth state had deposited its instrument of ratification with the Polish government. It has never been ratified by the USA who, whilst being signatories of the Protocol and prime movers in pressing for the meeting, still considered the limits too low.

2.2   MONTREAL AGREEMENT 1966/CAB 18900
Treaties are deemed to be permanent so when they are constructed rules are built in by which a contracting party can terminate its adherence in a formal manner should it so require. Such rules were incorporated into the Warsaw Convention. So the USA gave the obligatory six months notice − to expire in May 1966 − of their intention to withdraw from the Convention as a result of their concern that the value

of the limits of liability had been eroded by inflation. They subsequently retracted that notice, at a conference in Montreal, upon the acceptance by all carriers operating to or from the US, to give signed agreements (with the acceptance of their respective governments to the arrangement) increasing their liability where the Warsaw (or Hague) limits would otherwise apply, to US$75,000 inclusive of fees or US$58,000 exclusive of fees and waiving their rights of defence under Warsaw Article 20.

This became known as the **Montreal Agreement 1966** usually referred to under the US Civil Aeronautics Board reference number of **CB 18900.**

IATA was charged with the responsibility to work out the detailed provision including giving adequate notice to the public.

2.3   GUATEMALA PROTOCOL 1971

The debate generated by the Montreal Agreement led to the Guatemala City Conference and a further attempt to increase carriers liabilities, particularly as regards the level of compensation as required by the USA. An unusual condition was introduced into the wording relative to bringing the Protocol into force aimed specifically at circumventing the fiasco brought on by the failure of the US Senate to ratify the Hague Protocol. The Protocol is to come into force 90 days after the thirtieth instrument of ratification has been deposited; however, of those thirty it is laid down that five of the ratifications should account for at least 40% of the total scheduled air traffic, expressed in passenger-kilometres, for the year 1970 (per ICAO figures) which means without the ratification of the USA it is a non-starter. Since the USA has not ratified the Protocol it is not in force. (The Carriage by Air and Road Act 1979 empowered the UK to ratify the Protocol but this has not been done).

The Protocol makes major changes in the general scheme of carriers liability in respect of the carriage of passengers and baggage as follows:

(i)   the carrier is made absolutely liable for death of, or injury to, the passenger subject only to contributory negligence. In particular the defence available (Article 20(1) of Warsaw) that the carrier his servants and agents had taken all necessary measures to avoid the damage is removed (except where the liability is for delay).

(ii)   The maximum amount of the carriers liability is increased to:
Francs   1,500,000 for death or injury
Francs   62,500 for delay
Francs   15,000 for destruction of, damage to, loss of, or delay to passengers baggage.
Francs   250 per kilo for cargo

All limits exclusive of lawyers fees (Article 22 (3) (c) of Warsaw) .

(iii)   These limits are absolutely unbreakable in all circumstances. (e.g. defective documentation is no longer a loophole).

(iv)   The costs of the action are to be awarded in addition if, after six months from a written claim containing full particulars of the loss and calculations of the amount of the loss, the carrier has not made a written offer equal to the compensation awarded within the applicable limit.

(v)   The limit of 1,500,000 francs on claims for death or bodily injury would be raised by 187,500 francs at the end of the fifth and tenth calendar years after the coming into force of the Convention unless a two thirds majority at a conference held in those years agreed to a lesser or no increase.

(vi)   The date of conversion into local currency of the gold franc to be the date of settlement or court award and not the date of the accident.

(vii)   Suit may be additionally brought in accordance with Article 28 of Warsaw at a court of the domicile of the passenger if the carrier has a place of business in that country.

(viii)   A state may establish and operate **within its territory** a system to supplement the passenger compensation payable under the Convention:-

Subject to it not imposing any additional liability on the carrier.

Subject to it not imposing financial or administrative burdens in the collection of contributions on the carrier.

Providing it shall not give rise to any discrimination between carriers.

Providing that if a passenger has contributed to the system any person suffering damage as a result of the death or injury of that passenger shall be entitled to the benefits of the system.

2.3.1 Current Thinking on the Guatemala Protocol 1971

Inflation, the excessively low liability limits by modern standards and the changes in international monetary practice as to the use of the gold franc have major implications relative to the Warsaw Convention. Judicial interpretation of the Convention, amounting to rewriting of the text in some instances, threatens to destroy the uniformity which was its principal objective, in endeavours to award more to the plaintiff than the Convention would allow. As a United States District Court judge observed in Chan v Korean Air Lines arising from the disaster of September 1, 1983 (a judgement later adopted in full by the Court of Appeals):

"American courts, faced with the prospect of enforcing a limitation which has become outmoded and contrary to domestic law, have taken avoidance of the treaty limitation upon themselves and have arrived at an interpretation of the Warsaw system which (in some cases) eliminates the treaty limitation altogether".

The US Supreme Court subsequently rejected the opinions of the lower courts and restated the principle that courts are bound by the actual text of the Convention; but the quotation serves as an indication of the pressure for change.

A solution to defuse the pressure would be for the nations who have not done so to implement the Montreal Additional Protocols (which see), resolving the problems of the gold franc by substituting the SDR and the Guatamala Protocol 1971 to introduce absolute liability with increased and unbreakable limits for passengers and baggage (the Montreal Protocol No.4 does so for cargo).

Much talk takes place and even more drastic solutions have been advocated but no better hope immediately presents itself to speedily update the current international system of liability. The Lockerbie air disaster of 1988 in which many American citizens were killed drew fresh attention to the whole issue of limited liability and one assessment is that politically it reduced the likelihood of ratification of the Guatemala Protocol by the USA even with the advantage of an insurance plan.

2.4   MONTREAL ADDITION PROTOCOLS 1975

An international conference on air law was held in Montreal in September 1975 to consider amendment to the Warsaw Convention — as amended at the Hague — with the principal purpose of considering documentation and liability in respect of cargo and postal items (Additional Protocol No.4). In the event three further additional Protocols were agreed, each amending a different version of the Warsaw Convention, the main purpose being to make use of the concept of Special Drawing Rights rather than the Poincare gold franc in defining limits.

2.4.1 Special Drawing Rights

Special Drawing Rights (SDR) are an IMF unit of account. Originally they had a fixed value of 0.888671 grams of gold, hence one SDR equalled 15 Poincare gold francs. However, since 1978 they have had no link with gold and are based on a 'basket' of international currencies.

2.4.2 Protocol 1

This amended the limits of liability under the Warsaw Convention (Article 22) so that they became:

Passengers − 8,300 SDR's (or 125,000 monetary units equivalent to the gold franc).

Checked baggage and cargo − 17 SDR's per kilo (or 250 monetary units per kilo).

Unchecked baggage − 332 SDR's (or 5,000 monetary units) The SDR is that defined by the IMF to be converted into national currency at the IMF value for the SDR at the time of judgement. If the High Contracting Party is not a member of the IMF they may calculate the value in accordance with their own law, or if their law does not so allow then the monetary units mentioned may be converted into national currency in accordance with their laws. Each monetary unit is to represent 65 1/4 mg of gold of millesimal fineness of 900.

2.4.3 Protocol 2

This amended the limits of liability under the Warsaw Convention (Article 22) as amended by the Hague Protocol for passengers so that they became:

16,600 SDR's (or 250,000 monetary units)
(conversion to national currency as Protocol 1)

2.4.4 Protocol 3

This amends the limits of liability under the Warsaw Convention (Article 22) as amended by the Hague Protocol and the Guatemala Protocol so that they become:

Passengers − 100,000 SDR's (or 1,500,000 monetary units)

Delayed Passengers − 4,150 SDR's (or 62,500 monetary units)

Baggage − 1,000 SDR's (or 15,000 monetary units)

Cargo − 17 SDR's per kilo (or 250 monetary units per kilo)
(Conversion to national currency as Protocol 1).

2.4.5 Protocol 4

This amends the cargo provisions of Articles 5-16 of the Warsaw Convention as amended by the Hague Protocol. It also imposes strict liability on the carrier subject only to the following defences:

    (a)   inherent defect, quality or vice of that cargo.

    (b)   defective packing of that cargo performed by a person other than the carrier, his servants or agents.

(c)   an act of war or armed conflict

(d)   an act of public authority carried out in connection with the entry, exit or transit of the cargo.

The limit of liability becomes: 17 SDR's per kilo (or 250 monetary units per kilo) unless a special declaration of value is made and a supplementary sum paid to cover the increased limits of liability.

(Conversion to national currency as Protocol 1) Each of the above four Protocols to come into force 90 days after the deposit of the thirtieth ratification of that Protocol.

None of these are yet in force.

2.5   ROME CONVENTION 1933/LIABILITY TO PROPERTY ON THE GROUND

During the Warsaw conference in 1929 the question of liability for injury or damage to persons and property on the ground in some compulsory form was first raised but it was left to the Rome Convention in 1933 to try and establish a uniform system of law to cover this matter and it was here that the idea of compulsory insurance for such risks was introduced. The Convention did not receive much support and it was not until 1942 that the minimum of five ratifications had been made to give it effect; the UK was not one of them.

The Convention applies to both foreign and national aircraft, came into force on 13th February 1942 and provides for the prima facie liability of the aircraft operator which liability is limited to 250 gold francs per kilogram weight of the aircraft, every aircraft to be insured or guaranteed against such liability. Insurance is to be placed with an authorised insurer in the state of the aircraft's registration. The certificate or document of insurance is to be carried on board the aircraft. The **Brussels Protocol of 1938** tightened the insurance requirements to prevent insurers from seeking to avoid liability, though it did permit them certain defences.

2.5.1   Rome Convention 1952

There was a second **Rome Convention in 1952** coming into force 4th February 1958 (signed but not ratified by the UK and is unlikely to be so) relating to damage to persons or property on the surface, again with compulsory insurance requirements, similar in most respects but superseding and improving the previous Convention. Again the liability limit is based on gold francs (the same as in the Warsaw Convention) and the maximum take-off weight of the aircraft, and again a Certificate of Insurance must be carried (or a certified copy may be filed with the appropriate authority designated by the contracting state which is overflown).

Compensation requires proof only that the damage was caused by an aircraft in flight or by any person or thing falling therefrom. The liability attaches to the operator; however, if the operator did not have exclusive right to operate for a period not exceeding 14 days, then the registered owner will be jointly and severally liable with him. If the aircraft is used without the owners consent he will still be jointly and severally liable unless he can prove he exercised due care to prevent such unauthorised use. There is no liability if the damage is a direct consequence of armed conflict or civil disturbance or caused solely by the negligence or wrongful act of the person suffering damage. There is a Contribution Condition.

The limits for each aircraft and incident in respect of all persons liable are:

Maximum Take-off weight of aircraft.	Limits in gold francs
(a) up to 1,000 kgs:	500,000
(b) 1001 kgs to 6,000 kgs:	500,000 plus 400 per kg excess of 1,000 kg
(c) 6001 kgs to 20,000 kgs:	2,500,000 plus 250 per kg excess of 6,000 kg
(d) 20,001 to 50,000 kgs:	6,000,000 plus 150 per kg excess of 20,000 kg
(e) Excess of 50,000 kgs:	10,500,000 plus 100 per kg excess of 50,000 kg

The maximum liability in respect of loss of life or personal injury is 500,000 gold francs per person.

The liability becomes unlimited if damage is caused deliberately by the operator, his servants or agents. If the total amount of the claim exceeds the liability limitations, there are rules of distribution of the available funds between loss of life and personal injury on the one hand and property damage on the other with preferential treatment to the former.

2.5.2 Montreal Protocol 1978

In 1978 the Montreal Protocol amended the lower weight limit from 1,000 kg to 2,000 kg and the limits themselves from gold francs to SDR's (Special Drawing Rights as defined by the International Monetary Fund), at the same time substantially increasing them. This Protocol, however, has not yet received the necessary five ratifications and is consequently not in force.

Whilst the UK has not ratified the Rome Convention its air transport licensing conditions ensure that operators effect suitable insurance against damage to persons or property on the surface, and in English law itself there is provision for liability on the part of an aircraft owner or operator for such damage without proof of negligence.

2.6 CHICAGO CONVENTION 1944

During the Second World War a conference was held in Chicago with a view to establishing a new basis for international civil aviation, it being by then obvious that the existing regional arrangements were inadequate. Too few nations had been parties to the Paris Convention of 1919 and world wide air transport had developed considerably in the 25 years since that first convention. The Americans, who convened the conference hoped to take advantage of their dominance of aircraft production during the war by enshrining in an international agreement their own ideas of an 'open skies' policy. They did not achieve this but the Conference (of which most nations are now signatories) did agree to two basic concepts; that every state had absolute power to regulate and control its own air space and that the regulations once promulgated had to be imposed upon all aircraft, foreign or otherwise, with equal fairness and no nation's aircraft should be favoured above the rest.

Signatories to the Convention agreed that civil aircraft of other signatories on non-scheduled international flights may fly over and stop for non-traffic purposes in their territory without prior permission. The contracted state retained rights to lay down routes that must be observed across their territory and to prohibit or impose special regulations in certain areas or to specify the only airports that might be used.

States might refuse to allow revenue flights but might not enter into an agreement giving privileges to one operator over another in its airspace.

Scheduled international operators can operate only in accordance with bilateral agreements between the states concerned, such as that between the UK and USA known as the Bermuda Agreement which nominated the carriers who can fly between the two countries, the numbers of flights and the points of their arrival and departure. The Convention established the International Civil Aviation Organisation (ICAO). Two additional agreements were made as appendages to the Chicago Convention:

2.7   THE TWO FREEDOMS AGREEMENT 1944
Known as The International Air Services Transit Agreement permits scheduled international air services to overfly the territory of another contracting state and land for non-traffic purposes.

2.8   THE FIVE FREEDOMS AGREEMENT 1944
Known as The International Air Transport Agreement permits scheduled international air services
— to fly across its territory without landing.
— to land for non-traffic purposes.
— to put down passengers, mail and cargo taken on in the territory of the state whose nationality the aircraft possesses.
— to take on passengers, mail and cargo destined for the territory of the state whose nationality the aircraft possesses.
— to take on passengers, mail and cargo destined for the territory of any other contracting state and to be able to put down same coming from any such territory.

States who signed the Convention but not the additional agreements require bilateral negotiations for such permission/authorisations.

In the UK the Chicago Convention was given the force of law by the Civil Aviation Act 1946, replaced by the Act of 1949 and subsequently upgraded by the Acts of 1968, 1971, 1978, 1982 and the Orders issued under their authority.

2.9   GUADALAJARA CONVENTION 1961
The Warsaw Convention and subsequent Protocols regulate the carriers liability to passengers and cargo unless a direct contract of carriage has been made. Frequently, however, aircraft are chartered by travel companies or freight forwarders who themselves enter the contract with the passengers and consignees of cargo; such travel companies or freight forwarders could not obtain the protection of the Convention's limits of liability.

A number of nations met in Guadalajara in 1961 with a view to extending the Convention to establish rules for carriage other than by contracting carrier.

The Convention first defined the Contracting carrier to mean a person who as a principal makes an agreement for carriage governed by the Warsaw Convention with a passenger or consignor or with a person acting on behalf of a passenger or consignor.

It defined the Actual Carrier to mean a person, other than the contracting carrier, who by virtue of authority from the contracting carrier, performs the whole or part of the carriage contemplated but who is not with respect to such part a successive carrier within the meaning of Warsaw. Such authority to be presumed in the absence of proof to the contrary.

The Convention then agreed that when an actual carrier performs whole or part carriage which is international carriage according to the Contract made between the Contracting carrier for the whole of the carriage and the actual carrier both are subject to the rules of the Warsaw Convention.

Where a right for damages arises a claim may be made against either the actual or contracting carriers or both — the option being the plaintiffs but where either type of carrier is sued alone he is entitled to require that the other be joined in the proceedings.

Before legal action may commence written complaint must have been made to either one of the carriers within the time scale laid down by Warsaw.

The action must be brought either in a court where the contracting carrier may be sued or in a court where the actual carrier is ordinarily resident.

The two types of carrier are each liable for the acts and omissions of the servants or agents of the other but only when such servants or agents are acting within the scope of their employment and the act or omission relates to carriage performed by the actual carrier. Where the actual carrier is so liable he has benefit of the limits of the Warsaw Convention. Where the contracting carrier is liable for acts or omissions of the servants or agents of the actual carrier in circumstances where provisions for limited liability do not apply, both types of carriers lose the protection of the limitation of liability.

Unless he has agreed to them, any modification to his legal obligations or waiver of his rights made by the contracting carrier will not affect the actual carrier. Though the plaintiff can sue either or both types of carrier the aggregate amount recoverable is not to exceed the greatest amount which could be recoverable from either one and no person shall be liable for more than the limit which applies to him.

The rights of the two types of carrier as between themselves are unaffected by this Convention.

The Convention received the necessary five ratifications (including the UK's) and came into force in 1964. It was brought into UK law by the Carriage by Air (Supplementary Provisions) Act 1962.

2.10 **TOKYO CONVENTION 1963**

Proscribes not only ordinary criminal offences but also those which may or do jeopardise the safety of the aircraft or persons or property on board or which jeopardise good order and discipline on board. Acts of a political nature are excluded as are acts based on racial or religious discrimination and offences against military, customs or police aircraft.

The offence must have been committed on board an aircraft registered in a contracting state whilst that aircraft was in flight, or on the surface of the high seas or on ground which is not within the territory of any state.

The state of registration of the aircraft is said to be competent to establish jurisdiction but it has neither exclusive nor prior rights which may also be exercised by the state in whose airspace the offence has been committed, the state of nationality of the offender or of the offended upon, or the state whose security is threatened.

The Convention grants special powers to the aircraft commander whilst the aircraft is in flight, except over the state of registry unless the last point of take off or the next point of landing is outside the state of registry and on the ground following a forced landing until such time that the state authorities take over responsibility for the aircraft and the persons and property on board.

The special powers are:

2.10.1 Restraint

If the aircraft commander has reasonable grounds to believe that a person has committed or is about to commit an offence aboard his aircraft, jeopardising safety or good order on board, he may take reasonable measures including restraint to protect the safety of the aircraft and that of persons and property on board, to maintain good order and discipline or to enable him to hand over the person to competent authorities or disembark him. Crew members may be authorised or required and passengers may be authorised or requested to assist in imposing, such restraint.

Restraint must normally cease on landing; the state of landing must, therefore, if possible be given details of the occurrence before landing. Restraint may continue, however, if the aircraft lands in the territory of a non-contracting state whose authorities refuse to permit disembarkation of the alleged offender, of it the restraint has been exercised to enable the commander to deliver the alleged offender to competent authorities, of if a forced landing is made and the commander is unable to deliver the alleged offender to the competent authorities of if the alleged offender agrees to onward carriage under restraint.

2.10.2 Disembarkation

The commander has wide discretionary powers to disembark a passenger in any state in which his aircraft lands if he has good reason to think that the passenger has or is about to commit an act jeopardising good order and discipline or safety on board. Contracting states agree to allow such disembarkation and have no say in adjudging whether the disembarkation is reasonable — no provision is made for the subsequent onward cost of the carriage of the passenger.

2.10.3 Delivery

A commander with reasonable grounds to believe that a person has committed on board his aircraft an act which is, in his opinion, a serious offence under the law of the state of his aircraft's registration may hand over that person to the competent authorities in any contracting state in which the aircraft lands to whom he must also supply any evidence in his possession of the act itself. Contracting states undertake to accept delivery of such persons.

2.10.4 Immunity

A person against whom action has been taken in accordance with the Convention, as above, may not sue the aircraft commander, nor the aircraft owners, nor any passenger or member of the crew nor the operator or the person on whose behalf the flight was performed.

2.10.5 Preservation of Control

Under the Convention contracting states agree to take all appropriate measures to restore or preserve the commander's control of the aircraft — in the event of Hi-

Jacking the authorities of the state in which the aircraft lands must allow the passengers and crew to continue their journey as soon as practicable and return the aircraft and its cargo to the rightful owners.

Though this Convention is in force many states have yet to ratify it — though the USA did so in September 1969 and the UK brought it into law under the Tokyo Convention Act 1967, part activated by the Tokyo Convention Act (Commencement) Order 1968. (The second part of the Convention dealing with extradition has yet to be activated).

The Act also contains the provisions relating to piracy contained in the Geneva Convention on the High Seas 1958, referring to the definitions of acts of piracy and applying them to UK registered aircraft. Piracy takes place when the crew or passengers by any means direct activity against another ship or aircraft. It is included so that no doubt may arise as to the jurisdiction of any court in the UK.

2.11 HAGUE CONVENTION 1970

Hi-Jacking had not previously been legally defined in most countries. This Convention makes it an offence, on board an aircraft in flight, unlawfully by force or by other form of intimidation, to seize or exercise control of the aircraft, to attempt to do so, or to be an accomplice in such offence or attempt. Flight for the purposes of the Convention is from the time the external doors are closed after embarkation until they are opened for disembarkation. The Convention does not apply unless either the place of take-off of the place of actual landing is in a state other than the state of registration of the aircraft.

There was pressure to make this an offence subject to automatic extradition but the UK and some others declined to extradite political offenders. The Convention therefore says that states may either extradite the offender or refer the case to the prosecuting authority which in the UK is the Director of Public Prosecutions.

The Convention was given the force of law in the UK by the Hi-Jacking Act 1971 — which additionally states that the Act does not apply to aircraft used in military, customs or police service except when the offence is committed by a citizen of the UK or the Colonies or a British Subject, or if the Hi-Jacking takes place in the UK or the aircraft is registered in the UK or used in UK military, customs or police service. The Hi-Jacking Act 1971 was subsequently replaced by the Aviation Security Act 1982 which consolidated this and various enactments relating to aircraft/airport security, including inter alia, the Protection of Aircraft Act 1973 that had amended the 1971 Act and brought into force in the UK the Montreal Convention 1971.

2.12 MONTREAL CONVENTION 1971

This Convention, as supplemented by the 1988 Protocol, makes it an offence:

—   unlawfully and intentionally to perform an act of violence against a person when that person is on board an aircraft in flight and that act is likely to endanger the safety of the aircraft or that person is at an airport serving international civil aviation and the act is likely to cause serious injury or death.

—   to destroy an aircraft in service or so to damage it as to make flight unsafe or impossible.

—   to place or cause to be placed on an aircraft in service by whatever means a substance likely to destroy it or to so damage it that it cannot fly or that its safety in flight is likely to be endangered.

—   to destroy, damage or interfere with the operation of air navigation facilities with the result that the safety of an aircraft in flight is endangered.

—   to communicate knowingly false information thereby endangering the safety of such an aircraft.

—   to destroy or damage the facilities of an airport serving international civil aviation or damage aircraft not in service located on such an airport or disrupt the services of such an airport.

To attempt to do any of these things is also an offence as it is also to be an accomplice in such offence or attempt.

The contracting states must make these offences subject to severe penalties and must either extradite the offender or refer the case to the prosecuting authorities of the state where the offence took place.

2.13 MULTIMODAL TRANSPORT CONVENTION (GENEVA 1980)

Encouraged by the growth of the use of containers of uniform size the Convention covers the transport of goods by at least two different modes of transport on the basis of a multimodal contract from a place in one country at which the goods are taken in charge by the multimodal operator to a designated place of delivery in a different country. The Convention stipulated the issue of a multimodal transport document, specified its content and introduced a limited liability for loss of or damage to the goods by the operator expressed as not exceeding 900 units of account (uoa) per package or 2.75 uoa per kilogram gross weight whichever is the higher. If no water transport is involved then the operators limit of liability becomes 8.33 uoa. The Unit of Account (uoa) is the SDR (Special Drawing Right). If the state is not a member of the IMF the limits of liability are:

920	uoa	=	13,750	monetary units
2.75	uoa	=	41,25	,, ,,
8.33	uoa	=	124	,, ,,

(The monetary units are those used by the Warsaw Convention).

The UK has not ratified this Convention and is not likely to do so. Commercial practice is to use, where necessary, one of a number of published sets of conditions of contract, especially those preferred by the International Chamber of Commerce.

2.14 UK NATIONAL LEGISLATION (LEGAL LIABILITIES)

The Warsaw Convention was originally given the force of law in the UK by the Carriage by Air Act 1932, which was repealed under provisions within the Carriage by Air Act 1961 which introduced the Hague Protocol amendments though it did not come into force until an Order in Council was made in 1967. Meantime the Carriage by Air (Supplementary Provisions) Act of 1962 was passed dealing with the meaning of the term 'carrier, and bringing into English law the Guadalajara Convention rules subject once again to an order in Council being made to that effect. The Act enables the court to make any order it deems just and equitable to adjust the liabilities between the contracting and actual carriers.

2.14.1 The Carriage by Air Acts (Application of Provisions) Order 1967

This is the order in Council bringing the above two Acts into force (and applies also the Guadalajara provisions of the 1962 Act to all non international carriage to which the order relates).

The Warsaw Convention and its various protocols had dealt solely with international carriage as defined therein. The 1967 Order also applied the terms of the Warsaw Convention (as modified by the Hague Protocol) also to carriage **not** subject to that Convention (i.e. to internal flights). The Order, in schedule 2, recognises the continued existence of the Warsaw Convention for international carriage to those countries which, though having signed the Convention, have not signed the Hague Protocol. For carriage governed by the Hague Protocol the 1961 Act applies. For non-international flights the 1967 Acts introduce a new limit of liability of 875,000 gold francs. The carrier is made liable for the carriage of mail and postal packets with a limit of 250 gold francs per kilo.

Gratuitous carriage by air transport undertakings and the Crown are made subject to the Order; other forms of gratuitous carriage, namely private flights, are not governed by the 1961 Act nor this Order but by the ordinary principles of Common Law. Neither failure to issue a ticket nor a defect in the ticket issued expose the carrier to unlimited liability (though Warsaw and Hague would).

However, it is necessary, in order to limit his liability for baggage, for the carrier to record the number and weight of the bags — a prudent carrier therefore issues combined passenger and baggage tickets on internal service and charter flights.

The Order permits the Secretary of State to exempt as he thinks fit any carriage or class of carriage, or a person or class of person from any of the requirements imposed by the Order.

This power was initially of considerable importance to flying clubs who, in the case of proprietary clubs were able on receipt of exemption to obtain disclaimers from their members waiving any claims against the club. The exemption rendered the procedures valid and the waivers reduced the club's requirements in terms of liability insurance. The Unfair Contract Terms Act of 1977, with its prohibition of the exclusion of liability for death or personal injury by contract made this practice ineffective and the flying club exemption was withdrawn. As to member clubs, where the aircraft are owned in common by the members, the situation is untested in law but it is arguable that the terms of the 1977 Act do not apply.

2.14.2 Carriage by Air (Sterling Equivalent) Orders

The Minister is empowered to make orders from time to time giving the sterling equivalents of the value of gold francs mentioned in Warsaw (Hague).

The current order is the Carriage by Air (Sterling Equivalent) Order 1986, giving the following equivalents:

gold francs	sterling £
250	13.63
5,000	272.67
125,000	6,816.68
250,000	13,633.40

It is not necessary for the Order to specify the sterling equivalent of 875,000 gold francs as the Carriage by Air Acts (Application of Provisions) Second Amendment Order 1979 expresses the limits for non-international carriage in SDR's instead of gold francs (100,000 SDR's instead of the 875,000 gold francs).

2.14.3 Hovercraft Act 1968

This Act enables orders in Council to be made relative to both the operations of hovercraft and the third party liability of their operators. The Hovercraft (Civil Liability) Order 1986 regulated what those liabilities would be by using both aviation and marine legislation. For passengers and baggage the Carriage by Air Act 1961 and Carriage by Air (Supplementary Provisions) Act 1962 apply with certain modifications. The carrier is liable for injury or death to passengers and for loss of or damage to their baggage unless he proves he took good care. There is a limit of £30,000 in respect of passenger liability except in the case of wilful misconduct. For cargo the Carriage of Goods by Sea Act 1971 applies, again with modification, and that Act's liability limit per package or unit is used. For Third Party Liability the Merchant Shipping Act 1979 and the Merchant Shipping (Liability of Shipowners and Others) Act 1959 apply, again with modification. Hovercraft owners liability to third parties may be limited by reference to the hovercraft's maximum authorised weight in respect of property and injury or death caused to persons not on board the hovercraft providing the hovercraft is at the time of the incident over navigable water or in another maritime environment.

2.14.4 The Carriage of Goods by Sea Act 1971

As made applicable to hovercraft this act imposes certain obligations on the carrier including the requirement to exercise due diligence to make the hovercraft fit for the voyage and to supply a competent crew and service equipment. For cargo, the shipper can demand and must be given a bill of lading showing the marks necessary to identify the goods, the number of packages or pieces, or the quantity or weight as may have been given in writing by the shipper, the apparent order and condition of the goods.

Notice of loss or damage must be given in writing to the carrier or his agent at the port of discharge before or at the time the goods are removed but three days from the date of removal are allowed where the loss or damage is not apparent.

The carrier is not liable for loss or damage due to the unfitness of the hovercraft for the voyage except where that unfitness results from a lack of due diligence on his part. The following also enable the carrier to escape liability.

(i)   Act, neglect or default of the captain or crew in the navigation or management of the hovercraft.

(ii)   fire or any perils of the sea.

(iii)   Act of God.

(iv)   War, strikes, riots, civil commotions.

(v)   insufficient packing or latent defects.

2.15 NATIONAL VARIATIONS

It will have been noted that to be effective each Convention or Protocol requires ratification by individual states each of which then incorporates it into their own nation's law (as the UK did with Warsaw/Hague by act of Parliament, though under the codified system of law used in the rest of Europe, ratification usually automatically incorporates a Convention in its entirety into that particular country's law). It may well not appear in that nation's law in exactly the original text nor have exactly the same meaning (it will be remembered, for example, that the French word 'doll in the Warsaw Convention has no absolute translation into English, a problem removed by the Hague Protocol). Add to the foregoing the manner in which each national judicial system has developed in its own different way and it will be understood that the likely results of a certain course of action might vary from jurisdiction to jurisdiction, particularly between those systems based on Common law, e.g. UK and USA, and those based on Roman Law (Napoleonic Code in France), e.g. most of Europe. Shown below are some examples of national variations in the application and requirements of air law, starting with the USA which has more aircraft registered and flying than any other country and is the world's major aircraft manufacturer.

2.15.1 USA

The basis of law in the USA is similar to that in the UK being based on the old Common Law with the exception of the State of Louisiana which has a codified system reflecting its French ancestry. However, the USA consists in total of fifty states grouped together under a federal umbrella and each has its own legal system. (The basic system will be described in fuller detail in a subsequent section of the book). Each has developed that system away from the common root and in acknowledgement of this each state has its own conflict of laws rules though fortunately the development of law has followed a great degree of similarity in many states. The main differences lie in each state's interpretation of public policy and the fact that just a few have statutes limiting the amount of indemnity claimable by a victim after an aircraft accident. That list is diminishing but presently includes Kansas, Massachussetts, Missouri, New Hampshire, Virginia and West Virginia. Each state has its own Statute of Limitations. Given an aircraft accident of an international nature involving residents of different states, lawsuits can arise in several different jurisdictions which proceedings are then further complicated by the decision on the type of court and forum for the action. It is the plaintiff's legal advisers who choose and they will look for the jurisdiction where they feel they can do best and will join as many others in the action as possible, particularly the manufacturer of the aircraft, partly to include a defendant in the desired area of jurisdiction thereby obtaining access to that area and partly in the case of the aircraft manufacturer, to attempt to prove the liability against, and consequently obtain compensation from, a party not subject to limitation of liability.

In some states there are statutes in force that allow a plaintiff to instigate proceedings directly against the defendant's insurers.

When a number of US citizens are involved in a single accident anywhere in the world legal proceedings can be, and are, instigated in a number of different states, resulting in a multiplication of all the examinations, statements, costs and time taken.

In 1968 the US Congress passed the Multidistrict Litigation Act with rules of procedure to enable cases to be transferred to a single district for coordinated or consolidated proceedings, but for trial to be remanded at the district from which they came. This is a federal statute and applies only to cases brought in federal courts and not to those brought in state courts.

The Warsaw Convention, being applicable to international carriage, does not apply to domestic accidents in the USA. Regulations brought into effect in 1982 (23rd February) concerning all US Air Carriers (except on-demand air-taxi carriers and certain commuter carriers) apply also to all 'foreign' air carriers flying into or out of the United States and impose a requirement for compulsory insurance to minimum levels as follows:

(i)   bodily injury (excluding passengers) and property damage US $300,000 per person, US $20,000,000 per occurrence (US $2,000,000 per occurrence for aircraft of not more than 60 seats or 18,000 lb. overall maximum payload).

(ii) passengers US $300,000 per passenger times 75% of the installed seats in the aircraft per occurrence.

(iii) alternatively a single limit sufficient to cover the combined minimum required under (i) and (ii) above.

If there is a loss excluded by the policy to which the airline cannot respond financially then the insurers must do so and then seek recourse from the airline if they so desire.

(Federal Regulations Part 205 — see also London Market Clause AVN 57).

Third Party Liability in respect of injury to or death of persons and damage to property on the ground is normally brought under the Common Law but a few states have statutes in force which impose absolute liability on aircraft operators and two, New York and Michigan, have vicarious liability statutes through which the owner of an aircraft may be held liable for damage caused by the user.

2.15.2 SWITZERLAND (and for the purposes of aviation matters and the following notes: LIECHTENSTEIN)

Switzerland ratified the Warsaw Convention in 1934 and the Hague Protocol in 1962. It has signed and ratified the Guadalajara Convention of 1961 and all four of the 1977 Montreal Protocols. It has signed and ratified the Chicago Convention of 1944 and signed but not ratified the Guatemala Protocol and the Rome Convention.

Compulsory insurance is not at present required for passenger liability nor for liability towards other aircraft in the air nor persons travelling in such aircraft, but under Air Navigation Act 21st December 1948, Air Navigation Decree 14th November 1973, it is compulsory to insure against third party legal liability towards persons and/or property on the ground. The Acts do not limit liability but do impose minimum compulsory limits for which various aircraft must be insured. Up to these limits, shown below, the only exclusion permitted is in respect of War. The policy must not, therefore, other than excess of the minimum requirements, exclude any other risk, e.g. noise, pollution etc.
Limits current at December 1989

	Minimum amount to be covered by insurance, any one accident
	Swiss Francs
Aeroplanes and Helicopters up to 2,000 kg take-off weight.	2,000,000
Aeroplanes and Helicopters over 2,000 kg up to 5,700 kg take-off weight.	4,000,000
Aeroplanes and Helicopters Over 5,700 kg up to 20,000 kg take-off weight.	10,000,000

Helicopters Over 20,000 kg take-off weight.	40,000,000
Aeroplanes Over 20,000 kg up to 200,000 kg take-off weight.	40,000,000
Aeroplanes Over 200,000 kg take-off weight	60,000,000
Gliders and Motor Gliders	2,000,000
Balloons with Crew	2,000,000
Parachute Jumpers	1,000,000
Hang Gliders	1,000,000
Kites, Unmanned Balloons, Kite Parachutes and captive balloons	500,000

For any air borne or space vehicle or object, not included in the above list, the Federal Office for Civil Aviation will specify the amount to be insured on a case-by-case basis.

Though it is not compulsory to insure against passenger liability the legal requirement of indemnity remains, the Warsaw Convention having been incorporated into Swiss National Law by the 1948 Aviation Act and the various decrees. Rules are also to be found in the Code of Obligations, the Code of Insurance Contracts and the Code of Sickness and Accident Insurance.

2.15.3 Italy

Italy ratified the Warsaw Convention in 1929 and the Hague Protocol in 1963. It did not sign, but does adhere to the Guadalajara Convention of 1961. It has ratified all four of the 1977 Montreal Protocols. It has signed and ratified the Chicago Convention of 1944, the Rome Convention of 1952 and the Guatamala Protocol.

The main principles governing domestic carriage are contained in Articles 940 – 1000 of the Codice della Navigavione of 1942 which are substantially similar to the provisions of the Warsaw Convention with an additional liability placed upon a carrier if he fails to perform the carriage. It is also possible for the plaintiff to include a count for moral damages and for grief suffered as a result of an accident causing injury in his claim against the carrier.

The current legislation governing the limitation of liability in the international carriage by air of passengers is law 274/1988, applicable to all scheduled or non-scheduled flights to, from or with an agreed stopping place in Italy (it may also apply to on-carriage and also to tickets sold in Italy for flights not touching Italy at all). It requires a limit of SDR 100,000 per passenger to be included in the carriers general conditions with evidence of insurance up to this limit.

The Navigation Code also governs liability for damage to third parties on the ground with a compulsory insurance requirement based on the Rome Convention.

2.15.4 Federal Republic of Germany

Germany ratified the Warsaw Convention in 1933 and the Hague Protocol in 1960. It signed and ratified the Guadalajara Convention of 1961 but has not signed any of the four Montreal Protocols of 1977. It has signed and ratified the Chicago

Convention, has signed but not yet ratified the Guatemala Protocol; it has not signed the Rome Convention of 1952. Liability is governed by the German Air Navigation Law — Luftverkehrsgetz, broadly based on Warsaw though it has a more extensive definition of the word 'accident' and does not recognise claims for delay which are governed by the German civil code and can be modified by the carriers conditions of carriage. The Luftverkehrsgetz also compels German carriers to carry passenger accident insurance in the sum of DM 35,000 covering death and permanent disablement (which can be offset against any passenger legal liability award subsequently made). Foreign carriers intending to take on board new passengers in Germany must also first produce evidence that they carry this same insurance which is to apply when the passenger enters the aeroplane and ends when the passenger leaves it. It is also to be valid for the return flight of new passengers taken on board in the Federal Republic of Germany and must be paid even if a legal liability does not exist.

Although Germany has not ratified the Rome Convention the Luftverkehrsgetz imposes absolute liability for third party damage on the ground with a limitation according to the weight of the aircraft. However, if such damage is caused by the negligence of the operator or his agents unlimited liability applies.

CHAPTER 3

MANUFACTURERS LIABILITY

Because of the development of the law of tort, the increasing ability of investigators to pin-point the exact cause of a crash and the limitations of the Warsaw convention restricting the compensation available to plaintiffs, there is an increasing likelihood in the event of an aircraft accident for the manufacturer to be joined as a defendant in the legal action or sued directly as an alternative to the carrier. The liability of someone who creates or adds to or alters goods is not limited to a contractual basis. Both in the UK and the USA in the last century the Common Law has developed a recognition and definition of tortious liability arising from these activities. A claim can be made against either the main manufacturer or the maker of the individual part which is identified as being the cause of the accident.

In the USA the doctrine of strict liability is firmly established though variable to an extent between jurisdictions; in the UK, urged on by EEC directives, it is still under development. With strict liability it is not necessary to prove negligence on the part of the defendant but only to prove that the product was being used in the intended way and that as result of a design or manufacturing defect injury was suffered.

Claims against manufacturers fall mainly under the headings of:

failure to exercise reasonable care in design; negligence in the selection of material and the specifications of components; faulty construction/defective workmanship; shortcomings in the testing programme, including final check-out of the finished product.

3.1 CONSUMER PROTECTION ACT 1987

In the UK under the Consumer Protection Act 1987 the manufacturer is still able to bring forward certain defences in respect of a product:

(a) that the defect is attributable to compliance with any requirement imposed by or under any enactment (including Air Navigation Orders);

(b) that he did not at any time supply the product to another;

(c) that his only supply of the product to another was otherwise than in the course of a business of a defendant and that Section 2(2) of the Act does not apply to him, or applies to him by virtue of things done otherwise than with a view to profit. (Section 2(2) lists persons other than suppliers to whom liability may attach such as producers, those who hold themselves out as producers by marking the product, and those who import products into the EEC in order to supply them in the course of business).

(d) that the defect did not exist in the product at the relevant time.

(e) that the state of scientific and technical knowledge at the relevant time was not such that a producer of products of the same description as the product in question might be expected to have discovered the defect if it had existed in his products while they were under his control,

or (f) that the defect constituted a defect in a product (the subsequent product) in which the product in question had been comprised, and was wholly attributable to the design of the subsequent product or to compliance by the producer of the product in question with instructions given by the producer of the subsequent product.

Contributors negligence is also available as a defence.

(e)   above is usually referred to as the 'State of the Art' defence.

In the USA there is a growing body of authority favouring the availability of contributory negligence pleas in strict liability cases but in many jurisdictions this still will not hold as an ameliorating factor and effectively there are few, if any, other defences, the state of products liability law in the USA being in an extremely fluid situation.

CHAPTER 4

REGULATION OF FLIGHT

4.1   **CHICAGO CONVENTION**
In discussing the Chicago Convention of 1944 earlier, reference was made to the fact that the Convention was brought into law in the UK by various Civil Aviation Acts and the Orders issued under their authority.

4.1.1 **Aircraft registration**
It was the Chicago Convention that laid the international framework and basic standards for the world wide operation of aircraft though, since in the ordinary traffic flow it is irrelevant where the aircraft originally came from or is going to, most countries in formulating their national law to ratify the Convention made it applicable to internal flights as well. By the terms of the Convention every aircraft engaged in international air navigation must bear appropriate nationality and registration marks and such marks must be those of the state in which the aircraft is registered. An aircraft can only be registered in one country at any one time but the registration can be transferred from one country to another. Information concerning the registration and ownership of any particular aircraft must be given on request to any other contracting state or to the ICAO (Each country has its own unique prefix to the registration code that it gives to civil aircraft and it is required that the registration be displayed on the aircraft in a size and in positions designated).

4.1.2 **Facilitation of Flight**
Each contracting state agrees to issue regulations to facilitate and expedite the international passage of aircraft. They undertake to provide as far as they find practicable all facilities in accordance with recommendations made from time to time though it is accepted that not all countries can afford to provide the very latest air navigational/air traffic control aids.

4.1.3 **Documents to be Carried**
The Convention was concerned to ensure the safe and orderly growth of international civil aviation throughout the world, a phrase embodied in the constitution of ICAO, and to that end required that every aircraft should carry:

a certificate of registration.

a certificate of airworthiness.

the appropriate licences for each member of the crew.

a journey log book.

a radio station licence (if it is equipped with a radio).

a cargo manifest and detailed declaration of the cargo (if cargo carried).

The Convention further gave thoughts to international standards in:

communications and navigation aids.

rules of the air and air traffic control.

requirements for airports and landing areas.

aircraft airworthiness.

crew licensing.

maps and charts.

customs and immigration procedures.

aircraft in distress and accident investigation.

4.1.4 ICAO
Better, however, than simply setting standards at a given point of time, the Convention established an organisation to continue the work into the future:

The International Civil Aviation Organisation (ICAO)

ICAO was established by Part II (arts. 43 – 66) of the Chicago Convention 1944, which also serves as its constitution. It came into being on 4th April 1947. (it is now a specialised agency of the United Nations and the most important body in international civil aviation). Its aims and objectives are 'to develop the principles and techniques of international air navigation and to foster the planning and development of international air transport so as to:

a)   ensure the safe and orderly growth of international civil aviation throughout the world;

b)   encourage the arts of aircraft design and operation for peaceful purposes;

c)   encourage the development of airways, airports and air navigation facilities for international civil aviation;

d)   meet the needs of the peoples of the world for safe, regular, efficient and economical air transport;

e)   prevent economic waste, caused by unreasonable competition;

f)   ensure that the rights of contracting states are fully respected and that every contracting state has a fair opportunity to operate international airlines;

g)   avoid discrimination between contracting states;

h)   promote safety of flight in international air navigation;

i)   promote generally the development of all aspects of international civil aeronautics.,

ICAO consists of a Council, an Assembly and a Secretariat. The Assembly is composed of representatives of all the contracting states and normally takes decisions on a majority vote. It elects the Council, delegates powers to them, controls finance, makes amendments to the Convention and liaises between the organisation and governments. The Council is a permanent body composed of the representatives of twenty seven contracting states who are elected every three years and who perform the detailed work of the organisation in fostering the aims of its constitution, including the provision of technical assistance, the collection of statistics, publishing navigational and construction guides and information and preparation of draft conventions, working normally through its system of committees.

4.2 CIVIL AVIATION ACT 1982

The latest of the Acts by which the Chicago Convention is incorporated into UK law is the Civil Aviation Act 1982.

4.2.1 Development, Safety and Efficiency

Part 1 – the Secretary of State is charged with various duties relative to developing civil aviation, the production of aircraft, the promotion of safety and efficiency in their use and research into questions of air navigation. Most of his duties are then delegated to the CAA (Civil Aviation Authority) whose existence was established by the Civil Aviation Act of 1971 and who took over at that time the functions of the Air Transport Licensing Board and the Air Registration Board. Its continuing existence is established by the 1982 Act. Powers are taken under the Act to give effect to the Chicago Convention and safety recommendations made by ICAO. Power is also taken to issue Air Navigation and other Orders including those for the investigation of accidents.

4.2.2 Aerodromes, Road Traffic Acts

Part II of the Act relates to Aerodromes and makes provision for the Ministry of Transport, by statutory instrument, to extend the provisions of the Road Traffic Acts to roads within designated aerodromes and the CAA to make bye-laws regulating the use or operation of aerodromes. For aerodromes owned or managed by a local authority the power to make such bye-laws is theirs, subject to confirmation by the CAA before they become effective.

4.2.3 Nuisance, Third Party Ground Damage

Part III deals with the regulation of civil aviation including certain duties of the CAA. Section 76 within this part is important as it protects the owner or operator of an aircraft from any action for trespass or nuisance provided that the flight is carried out at a reasonable height above ground, having regard to wind, weather and all circumstances of the flight and subject to adherence to air navigation regulations.

It provides that where any loss or damage is caused to any person or property on land or water by an aircraft in flight or any person or article falling therefrom, damages for the loss or damage are recoverable without proof of negligence from the aircraft owner (or hirer in the case of lease for fourteen or more days). The owner (or hirer) has a right of recourse against any other responsible person. The only defence to a claim is that the damage was caused or contributed to by the negligence of the person by whom the damage was suffered.

4.2.4 Wreck and Salvage

Part IV applies to aircraft the same rules and law of wreck and salvage as apply to surface vessels. It deals with design, construction and maintenance of aircraft, rights relative to the mortgage, detention and sale for unpaid airport charges, matters of jurisdiction and the powers of the commanders of aircraft.

4.2.5 Air Navigation and Airworthiness orders

Part V covers miscellaneous and general matters including enacting that the Hovercraft Act 1968 shall include this Act.

In accordance with the powers given to him under the Civil Aviation Act 1982 the Secretary of state issues detailed regulations from time to time relating to the registration, licensing, airworthiness and operation of aircraft in the UK and it is to these regulations (or their equivalent in other countries) that all aviation policies refer when they warrant that "the insured will comply with all air navigation and airworthiness orders and requirements issued by any competent authority....... "

The current such comprehensive regulation is the: –

4.3   AIR NAVIGATION ORDER 1989

4.3.1 UK Registration
Part I covers the registration of aircraft in the UK, recognition of foreign registrations, and the marking of aircraft (spelling out in Schedule 1 B the exact sizes and positions of the marks that must be carried).

It makes the statement that no aircraft shall fly in or over the UK (with certain specified exception relating to gliders, aircraft flying under 'B' Conditions (experimental test etc.) kites or captive balloons), unless it is registered in the UK, some part of the Commonwealth, a contracting state to the Chicago Convention 1944 or where there is special inter-governmental agreement.

Only certain categories of persons may hold a legal or beneficial interest in a UK registered aircraft:

(a)   the Crown (i.e. H.M. Government);

(b)   Commonwealth citizens;

(c)   citizens of the Republic of Ireland;

(d)   British protected persons;

(e)   bodies incorporated in some part of the Commonwealth;

(f)   firms carrying on business in Scotland.

An aircraft may not be registered in two countries at the same time, neither may the aircraft be registered in one part of the Commonwealth if it could be more suitably registered in another part.

The Order sets out the procedure for registering an aircraft with the information required to be entered into the register. The CAA is the authority for registration of aircraft. Every aircraft must carry nationality and registration marks as required by the law of its country of registration. It must not carry any marks that purport to indicate that it is registered in a country where it is not registered or that it is a state aircraft when it is not.

4.3.2 Air Operators Certificates
Part II covers the requirements relating to air operators certificates – no aircraft may be operated for the purposes of public transport without one. The CAA will grant a certificate if it is satisfied that the applicant is competent to safely operate the type of aircraft for flights and purposes stated in the certificate, having regard to their previous conduct, experience, equipment, organisation, staffing, maintenance and other arrangements and conditions as the authority thinks fit – which includes financial resources and insurance cover.

4.3.3 Airworthiness Certificates
Part III covers airworthiness and equipment aspects. It details how airworthiness certificates are to be issued and renewed, the keeping of technical logs, inspection, overhaul, repairs, replacement and maintenance, licensing of maintenance

engineers, equipment to be carried, the weighing of aircraft and determination of their centre of gravity. No aircraft may fly unless there is in force a Certificate of Airworthiness (C of A) issued under the law of its country of registration. However, for flights within the UK the following are exempted:

— gliders not being used for public transport of passengers or aerial work;

— balloons not being used for public transport of passengers;

— kites;

— aircraft flying to obtain or renew a C of A, test flying of prototype or experimental aircraft (A or B Conditions);

— aircraft flying under a special permit to fly issued by the authority.

4.3.4 ARB (Airworthiness Requirements Board)
The CAA is the only body empowered to issue a C of A in the UK, but it has a statutory duty to consult the ARB on all matters appearing to the CAA to be of significance as respects the standards of design, construction and maintenance by reference to which Certificates of Airworthiness for aircraft are to be granted, or renewed in pursuance of Air Navigation Orders and to consult the Board as to whether an aircraft of a new type satisfies the standards of construction and design required for the issue of such a certificate.

The CAA has a duty to consider all advice so given.

The Board shall consist of not less than twelve nor more than twenty persons appointed by the CAA, four of whom shall be nominees one each from bodies representative of:

manufacturers of aircraft;

operators of aircraft; insurers of aircraft;
pilots of aircraft.

(Paragraph 85 Civil Aviation Act 1982 — Schedule 11 of that Act — gives further details of the Constitution of the Board).

4.3.5 Categories of Use
Each C of A when issued must specify the category of purposes for which the aircraft may fly and it may only be flown for those purposes — the alternatives are:

Transport category (Passenger) — allows any purpose;

Transport Category (Cargo) — allows any purpose, other than the public transport of passengers;

Aerial work category — any purpose other than public transport;

Private category — any purpose other than public transport or aerial work;

Special category — any purpose, other than public transport, specified in the C of A but not including the carriage of passengers unless expressly permitted.

4.3.6 Certificates of Maintenance Review
No aircraft registered in the UK, for which a C of A in either the transport or aerial work category is in force, shall fly unless the aircraft, including its engines, equipment and radio is maintained in accordance with a maintenance schedule

approved by the authority and there is in force a certificate signed by a licenced engineer to that effect, one copy of which is kept in the aircraft.

Such certificates to be issued for a prescribed amount of flying or elapsed time and must show when the next maintenance review is due.

4.3.7 Aircrew
Part IV covers aircraft crew and their licensing. An aircraft may not fly without a duly licensed crew of the number required by the law of the country of registration.

For UK registered aircraft the following regulations apply:

An aircraft registered in the UK must carry a flight crew adequate in numbers with appropriate and valid licences to ensure the safety of the aircraft and satisfy the aircraft's C of A requirements.

If the aircraft is flying for public transport and weighs more than 5,700 kg it shall carry not less than two pilots.

If it is flying for public transport in circumstances where

IFR apply and weighs 5,700 kg or less and is powered by:

– one or more turbine jets;

– one or more turbine propeller engines and provided with a means to pressurise the personnel compartments;

– two or more turbine propeller engines and certificated to carry more than 9 passengers;

– two or more turbine propeller engines, certificated to carry less than 10 passengers and not provided with pressurisation of the personnel compartments unless it has a serviceable and authorised autopilot;

– two or more piston engines, unless it has a serviceable and authorised autopilot;

– then it shall carry not less than two pilots.

An aircraft engaged on a public transport flight flying more than 500 nautical miles in one leg and passing over a specified area must carry either a flight navigator in addition to the other crew or navigational equipment approved by the CAA and used in accordance with conditions made by the CAA. (The listed areas include those such as the Sahara and the Arctic).

When the order requires that the aircraft carries radio equipment a member of the crew must be a flight radio operator. In certain circumstances he must be in addition to the existing crew.

4.3.8 Cabin Crew
When a public service aircraft carries twenty or more passengers or may, in accordance with its C of A, carry more than thirty five passengers and there is at least one on board, the crew of the aircraft shall include cabin attendants. These shall be not less than 1 for every 50 or fraction of 50 seats installed in the aircraft. The Authority has the right to give permission for lesser numbers for specific flights. It also has the right to specify greater numbers where it appears to them expedient to do so.

4.3.9 **Validity and Renewal**

Part IV continues with the specifications of the various licences required dependent on the use and type of the aircraft, the grant, effect and renewal of licences, their validation and the requirement to keep a personal flying log. Schedule 8 to the Order lists the full categories of the different types of licence, their privileges and the ratings that may be included.

4.3.10 **Operation of Public Transport Aircraft**

Part V deals with the operation of public transport aircraft, the operations and training manuals required and the responsibilities of the operator and in particular states that the operator of a UK registered aircraft shall notpermit the aircraft to fly without:

(a)   appointing a pilot to be commander of the aircraft for the flight;

(b)   satisfying himself that all the radio stations and navigational aids along the intended route or any planned diversion therefrom are adequate for the safe navigation of the aircraft;

(c)   satisfying himself that all aerodromes to be used, including alternate aerodromes, are adequately manned and equipped to ensure the safety of the aircraft and the passengers. He is not required, however, to check on the adequacy of fire fighting, search and rescue, or other services needed following an accident.

The operator must ensure that all crew members are sufficiently trained and licensed to perform the flight.

4.3.11 **Loading/Dangerous Goods**

Part V deals with the loading of the aircraft and operating minima, the duties of the commander including those relating to the instruction of the passengers in the use of emergency equipment and the action they shall take in an emergency. It covers operation of radio in aircraft, minimum navigation performance, use of flight recording systems, towing of gliders, towing picking up and raising of people and articles and the dropping of articles and animals. It states that no aircraft shall carry munitions of war, unless written authority is given by the CAA, and no person shall carry or have in his charge any weapon on board an aircraft registered in the UK. No dangerous goods may be carried except those permitted by the regulations promulgated by the Secretary of State and loaded packed and marked in accordance with his requirements.

4.3.12 **Carriage of Persons**

Part V specifies the method of carriage of persons, the marking of exits and break-in points, and regulations relating to endangering safety of an aircraft persons or property, drunkenness in an aircraft, smoking therein, the authority of the commander, stowaways and finally, exhibitions of flying.

4.3.13 **Crew Fatigue**

Part VI deals with precautions against crew fatigue giving detailed regulations to ensure that operators give their crews sufficient rest after duty and warning the operator that he must ensure that no flight crew member is permitted to work for any period which may cause him fatigue and so endanger the safety of the aircraft and its passengers.

4.3.14 Documents Required to be Carried

Part VII deals with documents to be carried in an aircraft, their preservation and production and offences in relation to them.

4.3.15 Air Traffic Control

Part VIII deals with the licensing of Air Traffic Control officers and grants the Secretary of State powers to make regulations prescribing

(a)   the manner in which aircraft may move or fly;

(b)   the lights and signals to be shown by aircraft;

(c)   the lighting and marking of aerodromes;

(d)   air traffic control services to be provided at aerodromes;

(e)   any other safety regulations.

He may also, in the public interest, restrict or prohibit flying in the UK by reason of

(a)   the intended gathering or movement of a large number of persons;

(b)   the intended holding of an aircraft race or contest or an exhibition of flying;

(c)   national defence or any other reason affecting the public interest.

4.3.16 Aerodrome Licensing

Part IX covers the licensing of aerodromes and particularly the Secretary of State's powers to prescribe the conditions under which noise and vibration may be caused by aircraft at any aerodrome.

Part X covers various miscellaneous items, including powers and interpretations.

4.4   AIR NAVIGATION (GENERAL) REGULATIONS 1981

These stipulate what must appear on the load sheets required under the Air Navigation Order (Part V dealing with the operation of aircraft). They must include

(a)   nationality and registration marks of the aircraft;

(b)   details of the flight;

(c)   the total weight of the loaded aircraft;

(d)   the weights of the several items from which the total aircraft weight has been calculated;

(e)   the load distribution and the resultant position of the centre of gravity.

Article 4, apart from the above requirement, lays down the basis on which the total weight of any aircraft flying on public transport shall be calculated; gives standard weights to be used for passengers and crew in lieu of actual weight provided the aircraft has an authorised weight in excess of 5,700 kg or a total seating capacity of 12 or more passengers, and a standard method of calculating the weight of both cabin and hold baggage.

This regulation does not alter the laws relating to the issue of tickets/baggage checks nor the manner in which protection is obtained under the Acts affecting the carrier's limitation of liability.

The regulations permit certain noise and vibration to be caused by aircraft:

(a)   while taking off or landing;

(b)   when being moved on the ground or water;

(c)   as a consequence of the engines being operated

  —   to ensure satisfactory performance;

  —   for the purpose of raising the engines to their proper temperature in preparation for, or at the end of, a flight;

  —   for the purpose of checking that instruments, accessories, or components are in a satisfactory condition.

These regulations permit pilots and owners of aircraft in the general category to carry out certain repairs and replacements, mostly those not requiring special tools. In all circumstances the aircraft log books must be completed for such work.

4.5   UK RULES OF THE AIR AND AIR TRAFFIC CONTROL REGULATIONS 1985
This contains 10 sections.

Section 1 — interpretation, gives certain major definitions: 'Air Traffic Control Clearance' means authorisation by an air traffic control unit for an aircraft to proceed under conditions specified by that unit.

'Anti-collision light' means

(a)   in relation to a rotorcraft: a flashing red light;

(b)   in relation to any other aircraft: a flashing red or flashing white light;

and in either case they must show in all directions for the purpose of enabling the aircraft to be more readily detected by the pilots of distant aircraft.

'Apron' means the part of an aerodrome provided for the stationing of aircraft for the embarkation and disembarkation of passengers, the loading and unloading of cargo and for parking.

'Ground Visibility' means the horizontal visibility at ground level.

'Manoeuvering area' means the part of an aerodrome provided for the take-off and landing of aircraft and for the movement of aircraft on the surface, excluding the apron and any part of the aerodrome provided for the maintenance of aircraft.

Section 2 — General. Application of rules to aircraft, misuse of signals and markings, reporting hazardous conditions, low flying rules, simulated instrument flight and practice instrument approaches.

Section 3 — Lights and other Signals to be shown or made by aircraft.

Section 4 — General Flight Rules for avoiding collisions and aerobatic manoeuvres.

Section 5 — Visual Flight Rules

Section 6 — Instrument Flight Rules

Section 7 – Aerodrome Traffic Rules, aircraft movements, landing and take-offs, special rules for certain aerodromes.

Section 8 – Miscellaneous Special Rules. Cross Channel air traffic, upper flight information regions, Scottish terminal control areas.

Section 9 – Aerodrome Signals and Markings, Visual and Aural signals.

Section 10 – Air Traffic Control. To be provided in accordance with the Authorities requirements.

4.6 CIVIL AVIATION (INVESTIGATION OF ACCIDENTS) REGULATIONS 1989

This is an order in four parts:

Part I – imposes duties to furnish information relating to accidents, deals with the removal of damaged aircraft, the appointment of air accident inspectors and their powers, the form and conduct of investigations and the inspectors reports thereon.

Part II – deals with review boards, their appointment, proceedings and publication of reports.

Part III – deals with Public Inquiries.

Part IV deals with accidents to aircraft registered outside the UK, obstruction of investigations, provisions as to Scotland and Northern Ireland.

4.7 CIVIL AVIATION ACT (APPLICATION TO CROWN AIRCRAFT) ORDER 1959

This applies the 1951 regulations, predecessor of the 1969, 1983 and currently 1989 Aviation (Investigation of Accidents) Regulations – referred to above – to aircraft
belonging to the Crown.

4.8 THE CIVIL AVIATION AUTHORITY (CAA)

This was established by the UK Civil Aviation Act of 1971 by which authority it took over the functions, inter alia, of the Air Transport Licensing Board and the Air Registration Board. Its authority and functions are presently controlled by the UK Civil Aviation Act of 1982. Its duties include:

The licensing of air transport (including air travel organisers), the provision of air navigation services and the registration of aircraft.

Prescribing the minimum requirements for construction, workmanship and materials for an aircraft and issuing, when satisfied, the necessary certificate of airworthiness without which an aircraft may not fly (its authority includes the ability to revoke licences if the authority so thinks proper).

Issuing Certificates to air operators and licences to pilots, aircrew, aircraft maintenance engineers, air traffic controllers and aerodromes all in accordance with the powers granted to it, and provided the necessary requirements are satisfied.

For accident prevention the CAA has a mandatory system of occurrence reporting the information received being disseminated to manufacturers, operators and those who maintain aircraft and associated equipment. Accidents that do occur are analysed both in the UK and world wide with the aim of applying preventative measures. To that end they closely liaise with the Accident Investigation Branch (AIB) of the Department of Transport whose responsibility it is to investigate aircraft accidents in the UK. When the AIB inspectors discover a safety factor which they believe warrants urgent attention they inform the CAA so that the latter can consider taking action without waiting for the Chief Inspector of Accidents to publish his formal report.

4.9   AIR ACCIDENTS INVESTIGATION BRANCH (AAIB)

This is part of the UK Department of Transport, based at Farnborough, their task is the investigation of accidents arising out of civil aviation in the UK and British registered or manufactured civil aircraft abroad. They are responsible directly to the Secretary of State for Transport.

They additionally provide technical assistance in air accident investigations for the UK Ministry of Defence. In the USA, the broad equivalents of the CAA, ARB and AAIB, are the FAA, CAB and NTSB.

4.10   THE FAA (FEDERAL AVIATION ADMINISTRATION is now part of the Department of Transportation of the Government of the United States of America. Its duty, under the Secretary of that department, is to encourage and foster the development of civil aviation and air transport both in the USA and abroad, taking into account the requirements of national defence, the development of civil aeronautics, the control and use of navigable air space in the USA and the regulation of civil and military occupations in air space, including research, development, installation and operation of air navigation facilities.

Among other specifically delegated powers, the FAA also has powers to provide air transportation security, enforce minimum standards of safety (including setting qualifications for, and the issue of Certificates to, airmen and aircraft and the issuing of air carrier operating Certificates) and control and abate aircraft noise and sonic boom.

4.11   THE CAB (CIVIL AERONAUTICS BOARD)

This is an independent agency of the Government of the United States of America having broad economic regulatory responsibility which it must perform in accordance with public convenience and necessity.

It is the CAB who issues the necessary Certificate of Public Convenience and Necessity without which a US air carrier cannot operate nor indeed a foreign air carrier operate in their territory.

The previous power of the CAB to regulate safety and investigate accidents has been transferred to the US National Transportation Safety Board.

4.12   THE NTSB (NATIONAL TRANSPORTATION SAFETY BOARD)

This is an independent agency of the United States Federal Government, based in Washington DC. Its remit is to seek to assure that all types of transportation in the United States are conducted safely. The Board investigates accidents and makes recommendations to government agencies, the transport industry, and others on safety measures and practices. The Board also regulates the procedures for reporting accidents and promotes the safe transport of hazardous materials by government and private industry.

CHAPTER 5

THE USA

5.1 JURISDICTION

Certain aspects of the legal system in the USA have already been considered when looking at national variations in the development of air carrier legislation, as has also the question of compulsory insurance relative to third parties and passengers.

The term jurisdiction in reference to American Courts has two meanings; first the territorial one in that each state or district is a jurisdiction; secondly it has the meaning, relating to the right and authority of the court to entertain an action and to render a disposition of an action.

Jurisdiction in the latter sense comprises two separate elements. First, that known as subject matter jurisdiction is concerned with the authority of a court to entertain a particular type of action, regardless of the nature of the parties to the action. Every state has at least one trial court of unlimited jurisdiction which is competent to adjudicate any action and to render a judgement for any amount. Similarly the United States District Courts all have subject jurisdiction over actions arising under the laws and treaties of the United States and causes of action between citizens of different states and/or foreign citizens or corporations where damages claimed are in excess of a certain limit. The State Courts and the United States District Courts have concurrent jurisdiction in many instances and a plaintiff may have an option, guided by his lawyers, of where to initiate an action. Secondly, that known as jurisdiction over a party deals with the authority of a given court over a person or presence of a party to an action by reason of territorial considerations, for example in a products liability case a foreign manufacturer will not in theory be subject to the jurisdiction of a state unless he does business there or undertakes some purposeful activity to avail himself of the rights, privileges and protections of that state. It is, however, possible for the foreign manufacturer to be found to be transacting business in a state sufficiently to be subject to jurisdiction on any case of action; (i) if he places an article in the stream of commerce which causes injury within those jurisdictions; (ii) if that manufacturer distributed the product outside his own jurisdiction with a reasonable expectation that the product was capable of reaching and causing injury within the jurisdiction; (iii) if that manufacturer derives substantial profit from international commerce; or (iv) if that manufacturer consistently acts within the state and derives revenue from that state.

5.2 THE ATTORNEY

In Court, both sides will be represented by at least one attorney (unlike the UK which presently divides the legal profession into solicitors and barristers). The attorney in the USA acts in both capacities, his ability to appear in court only restricted by his licence. He is licensed by the state he operates in and can only appear in the state or federal district courts of that state; hence in the case of a major accident several law firms may well be involved to cover the several different jurisdictions in which actions are brought.

The US attorney, acting for a plaintiff, works not on a charge calculated on the time spent on the case as would his counterpart in the UK or as does the defendants attorney in the USA, but on what is known as a contingent fee basis (in the US, costs are not awarded against the defendant on the successful outcome of a plaintiff's case nor vice versa). Plaintiffs attorneys charge fees between 30% and 40% (usually 33 1/3%) of the total recovery made by the plaintiff; no cure no fee. The plaintiff has nothing to lose, the attorney everything to gain in prosecuting a case and ignoring realistic offers at an early stage.

5.3 LITIGATION PROCEDURE

The procedure commences with service of process, usually a summons and complaint, by the plaintiff's lawyer (attorney) to the defendant; drawn in the widest possible terms this document will name as many co-defendants as possible, including providing for additional defendants by using the expression Doe 1 (and as many other Doe's in numerical sequence that the attorney likes). Doe being the shortening of the expression John Doe used where the English would use A.N. Other. At this time the facts are not available to determine who really is involved and in what areas and to what extent. The idea is that at the end someone will pay.

The defendants response at this time can only be a general denial and an attempt to obtain more specific information. The next stage is 'discovery'; each jurisdiction has its own rules governing civil procedure and contained within these rules are the parameters within which discovery and deposition (written testimony of a sworn witness) may be made. The rules are broad. Essentially discovery is a system whereby, with the authority of the court, parties in litigation, particularly plaintiffs, can make searching investigations into documents, demand written and/or oral examinations of persons, physical or mental examination and the inspection of any property. The only restriction is that it must be relevant to the pending action — a condition that can be very widely interpreted.

A party being subjected to discovery can appeal to the court to have a limitation placed on the ground of irrelevance, but usually with little success. Discovery usually ascertains what insurance is behind the defendant, its limits and indeed can give the plaintiff sight of brokers and insurers files.

Whilst the plaintiff's attorneys are seeking the information and evidence they need to build their case, the defendants attorneys are working collecting documents, statements from witnesses and meeting with the plaintiffs attorneys to find out the actual accusations they will face and build the defence against them.

When the plaintiffs attorneys decide they have discovered all that they want they will have the case placed on the trial calendar and in due course the case will come to trial before judge and jury.

5.4 PUNITIVE DAMAGES

The question of awards to plaintiffs of punitive damages is one heard only in reference to complaints arising in the USA. It is a question that has been debated for a long time but is once again current with, at the time of writing, two decisions under appeal before the US Court of Appeal for the District of Columbia circuit which will almost certainly go from there to the supreme Court.

The first case arose out of the litigation on the Pan-Am/Lockerbie bombing and on the 3rd January 1990 Judge Platt held at the US District Court, New York Eastern District, that punitive damages were not recoverable under the Warsaw Convention, even on a showing of wilful misconduct, on the basis of the Supreme Court's recent ruling that only the political authorities have the power to repudiate or amend the Warsaw Convention and it must be interpreted in the only manner consistent with the shared expectations of the Contracting Parties at the time.

In the second case Judge Sprizzo of the US District Court, New York Southern District, in the litigation arising out of the Pan-Am/Karachi Hi-Jacking held not more than five days later that punitive damages were recoverable under the Warsaw Convention on a showing of wilful misconduct and stated that 'punitive damages are a part of Common Law tort remedies ...... and no language in the Convention pre-empts or precludes such claims.'

5.4.1 The Purpose of Punitive Damages

Punitive damages (or exemplary damages) have long been recognised in US Common Law, though they are a departure from the normal rule that it is irrelevant to the amount of damages whether the injury was deliberate or accidental, they are not an indemnity and are in excess of the true compensation for the injury done. Punitive damages are awarded to punish the defendant and express society's indignation at the outrage done to the plaintiff. They are supposed to act as a deterrent and warning to others against committing the same offence and are a revenge for the injured party. Most states have statutes/consumer protection acts allowing these awards often as part of a consumer-product safety standard regulation. Until recently, however, an area relatively free from such awards has been public international aviation law which has as its avowed purpose the uniform application of liability rules relative to international transportation by air.

Punitive damages are not awarded as a matter of right but at the discretion of the jury who base their decision on:

the grievousness of the act;

the degree of malicious intent;

the wrongdoers ability to pay.

The latter guide-line is something peculiar to most of the states of the US and takes into account the scale of the defendants insurance policies.

5.4.2 Limits

There is no limit to what punitive damages a jury can award and the sums involved often bear no comparison to a reasonable award. The courts have the power to set aside awards which are in their opinion excessive (which they can also do with compensatory damages); however, they invariably take the attitude that if the defendant does not like it he will have to appeal to a higher court to see if he can get it changed.

5.4.3 Right or Wrong?

Apart from the debate as to whether or not punitive damages are permissible under the Warsaw Convention, an underlying debate centres on whether they are right in themselves. They are a penalty, and a fine, and yet the defendant, because it is a civil action, is deprived of the safeguards available to him in a criminal action. He can also be criminally charged for the same act. Is it right also that the plaintiff should receive the punitive award? He has already been awarded his rightful damages in compensation, and much of it will go to his legal advisers. If it is a fine and an expression of society's indignation, should the money if awarded not go to society as any other fine would? They have no limits and bear no relationship to what is a reasonable award.

For the system it is argued that compensatory damages come from insurers, (a punitive award may not) and therefore is the true punishment and should make the defendant more careful in future. The threat of punitive damages also permits the plaintiff's lawyer to gain more in compensatory damages for his client.

5.4.4 Insurance Implications

Given that the defendant has had to pay punitive damages, the question then arises as to whether he can, or indeed should be able to, recover his payment from insurers. Should he be able to shift the burden of payment to an insurance company and negate the very purpose of punitive damages, i.e. punishment? If he can, is this socially acceptable, not just from the moral viewpoint, which is important, but also in that it will increase the cost of insurance to other consumers? Would not the knowledge that the 'deep pockets' of insurers were paying surely increase further the extravagant punitive awards made?

On the positive side, surely to leave the insured without cover is unacceptable and it must be unreasonable to deny employers cover who themselves are only vicariously liable. Most policies do not specifically exclude claims for punitive damages; most insured believe they are covered for them on the grounds that their policies state 'to pay on behalf of the insured all sums which the insured shall become legally obligated to pay as damages......' (AV 16). Is it not illogical to pay compensatory damages but to deny punitive damages? Would insurers who refuse to settle wrongful death claims when faced with seemingly exorbitant compensatory damage demands then be held accountable for exposing their insureds to punitive damage findings by US juries? Would the air carriers themselves be required to assume an adversarial stance with their insurers and retain independent attorneys to counsel them where 'wilful misconduct' is alleged? Will reinsurers pay for claims settled by reinsureds at amounts which clearly contemplate punitive damages? The position of insurers is difficult; in a very few states the law is clear and the insurability of punitive damages is against the public policy of those states. In the majority, however, there is no clear resolve, most of the case law having arisen from motor accidents and no decisions made in the field of aviation. One of the best known cases is that of a motor case that went before the Federal Appeal Court in Florida in 1962 (Northwestern National Casualty Co. v McNulty). The Court ruled it would not permit an insurer to be held liable for the punitive damages part of the judgement imposed as a deterrent or punishment on the insured driver. However, in other states the opposite conclusion has been reached on appeal.

The matter remains confused. Current aviation market practice is that on receipt of a complaint indicating a count of punitive damages, insurers put the insured on notice that they, the insurers, reserve their rights to say they will not be liable for the punitive damage award, if any, under their policies and that because their policy may not be able to respond, the insured should instruct his own attorney to defend this particular issue.

C H A P T E R 6

CLAIMS

6.1 Investigation and Handling

Upon the occurrence of a flying accident, the civil authorities must be informed. They will, in the majority of cases, undertake an investigation to discover the cause and will take action where possible to prevent a recurrence. They will almost certainly investigate if loss of life has been involved. The insured also has a duty to give immediate notice of any event likely to give rise to a claim under his insurance to the person named for that purpose in his policy (usually his brokers) who will in turn advise the underwriters.

The first need is for clear precise facts about the accident. On the basis of these the underwriters will normally appoint a qualified surveyor to act on their behalf and, if a major accident, represent their interests in the investigation. If third party damage has occurred or a passenger is involved underwriters may also instruct solicitors to handle the liability aspects, as they may also do if subrogation is a possibility in the event of an aircraft covered by them has been damaged by someone else. Once instructed by the brokers, acting on behalf of underwriters, the surveyor is expected to act with all speed; this is the proof of the insurance as far as the client is concerned. In the case of the hull where there may be the likelihood of some form of finance involved, such as lease, mortgage, or hire purchase, the payment structures may require the payments to go on even if the aircraft is not earning or until the total balance has been paid.

Upon investigating the accident the surveyor is expected to present his initial report to his principal (the underwriter) at the earliest possible moment, specifying all the facts he can gather including, briefly, the cause of the accident and if possible the estimated cost of repair. This initial report will help the underwriters to decide what, if any, further action to take.

6.2 SELECTION OF SURVEYOR

The underwriters initial selection of a surveyor to act for him will be influenced by a number of factors — his personal preference, what might have been agreed when the insurance was originally effected, the part of the world where the accident took place. There are throughout the world qualified surveyors ready and able to give good local service on light aircraft and even some of the larger general aviation aircraft. However, if a larger type of aircraft is involved or something possibly unusual they normally employ the services of one of the big international surveying organisations such as Airclaims Limited or Lloyd's Aviation Department. *SEARCH COMPANIES.*

6.2.1 Airclaims

Airclaims Limited is an international organisation with largely autonomous regional offices at strategic locations throughout the world and represented by field surveyors in many other areas. Airclaims, previously known as Aircar Limited, acquired the Air Safety and Survey Division of the British Aviation Insurance Company in 1970, since which time they have established comprehensive statistical and intelligence services for subscribing aviation insurers and aircraft operators including publishing a weekly Information Digest.

Airclaims provides surveys and assessments for and of aircraft operators and manufacturers, advice on safety and reports on accidents in nearly every part of the world.

6.2.2 Lloyd's Aviation Department

Lloyd's Aviation Department (LAD) started in 1946 and consists of two main sections;

Survey: the staff of which are surveyors who investigate aviation claims, estimate damage and check circumstances.

Information and Records: which produce Lloyd's Confidential Index and record and generally provide information on any aspect of aviation to Lloyd's underwriters.

6.3   SURVEYORS DUTIES

Although he acts with all speed, it is not always easy for the surveyor to get to the site of the accident. Internal travel may be difficult and he has no legal standing unlike the official investigators representing the airline, the manufacturers and the local civil aviation authorities. Nevertheless, he must endeavour to file his preliminary report as soon as possible together with any recommendations he feels able to make at that time. The surveyors task is to glean and report to underwriters the following details and as much background information as he can, usually supported by photographs:

Identification of the aircraft, its type and registration, the date of expiry of its C of A. The names of the pilots and other crew with full details of their licences and experience. Weather information during and before the accident, use of fuel, what the aircraft was doing, its load and weight and maximum permitted weight.

Maintenance history of the aircraft and engines. Communications with air traffic control. Opinion with regard to the cause of the accident, and, having examined the wreck, the extent of damage and cost of repair and/or possibilities of salvage.

Any further recommendations with regard to his findings should also be included.

6.4   HULL CLAIMS

Assuming the loss to be repairable and not total, the surveyor will in addition to investigation, normally be involved in watching over the repair and approving the repairers bills.

It is the underwriters claims adjusters job to satisfy himself that the loss is a valid claim under the policy underwritten. First, is the aircraft listed on the Slip and/or policy? Did the loss occur during the policy period, and in its geographical limits? Was the purpose for which the aircraft was being used permitted by the policy? Was the pilot a permitted pilot under the terms of the policy? Did the policy cover flight risks? Do any of the policy conditions or exclusions apply? Is the premium paid? If not a total loss, is the amount claimed reasonable? or if a total loss and there is not an Agreed Value on the policy is the proposed settlement amount neither more nor less than an indemnity, having regard, for example, that if the policy is written on form AVN 1A that the underwriter has the option to pay for, replace or repair the damage. Using recommendations given by the surveyor, the adjuster must take into account where repairs could most economically yet properly be arranged given the location and situation of the damaged aircraft and the probable costs of transport to repairers. What is the availability of spares?

If it is a total loss or the adjuster has decided that it should be deemed so, he is likely to pay cash (less any applicable deductible). The replacement option is rarely used as it is not at all easy to obtain a second-hand aircraft let alone in 'reasonably like condition'. The adjuster must now take into consideration, again possibly based on information received from the surveyor, or maybe later from an official accident report prepared by the civil authorities, whether there is a case for subrogation and, if so, instruct a lawyer accordingly.

For repairable losses on small aircraft it is worth bearing in mind that, since insurance is an indemnity, technically it is the responsibility of the policyholder to settle all repair accounts (after their approval by the surveyor) before being reimbursed by underwriters, though often insurers will negotiate with the repairers on the basis of paying them direct less the deductible which the insured himself must pay.

6.4.1 Brokers Duties

The initial advice of the claim is normally given to the broker involved. He will liaise between the surveyor and underwriter and in due course collect the surveyor's fees from underwriters and settle them to him. The broker will have advised not just the leading underwriters but all those, including the overseas markets, who subscribe to the risk and will alert them, if necessary, of the possibility that a special collection will be made should the loss being faced be that of a major aircraft.

In the event of a dispute over the claim the brokers responsibility is to negotiate his clients case.

6.4.2 Proof of Loss

Provided that all is in order and the underwriters have agreed to settle the loss, they obtain before doing so, from claimants anywhere in North or South America a document known as a Proof of Loss and the agreement to settle will be made subject to sight and approval of that document duly signed by the insured. (A Proof of Loss is a sworn statement by the named insured, setting forth his interest and that of all others in the property affected and encumbrance thereof. The amount, place, time and cause of the loss and the description and amounts of all other insurance covering the property, together with the name and certificate number of the pilot flying the aircraft).

The broker can now collect the claim from underwriters but finally, before money actually is paid to the insured, a check must be made of the slip/policy or possibly within the brokers records to ensure that it passes to the right recipient; for example there may be a Loss Payee clause part of a Hire Purchase or Lease Agreement or similar stipulating to whom the money should be paid in the event of a loss.

6.4.3 Ex Gratia

In certain circumstances underwriters may consider that they are not in fact liable to pay the claim submitted under their policy but will nevertheless do so where non-payment could be deemed a harsh decision or there is a good business connection involved and non-payment could sour relations. Such payments are known as ex gratia – as a gift – and would not generate rights of subrogation.

6.4.4 Sharing Agreements

If there is a separate war risks cover and there is doubt as to whether loss of or damage to the aircraft was caused by an accident or by a risk of war, the burden is on the 'All Risks' insurers to show that the claim is not under their policy before the insured can make his claim on the 'War Risks' insurers. This is not always an easy task. For example, despite much costly search and investigation the cause of the loss of the Indian Airlines Boeing 747 which came down into the Atlantic off Ireland in June 1985 has still not been established, so in theory four years later the insured could still be waiting for his money.

The market as a whole, aware of just such a possibility, and concerned about the inevitable bad publicity which would result, published in 1983 the Slip Clause AVS 103 variously known as The Cross Market Sharing Agreement; the Provisional Claims Settlement Clause; the 50/50 Clause (its true title is 50/50 Provisional Claims Settlement Clause (AVS 103)) which if, appearing on both the Hull 'All Risks' and 'War' slips ensures that the insured is paid, all else being equal, by the two markets each contributing 50% of the loss. It is then for the underwriters to settle between themselves how the issue should finally be resolved and on whom the loss should eventually fall.

6.5   LIABILITY CLAIMS

The initial procedures adopted by the broker and the reactions of the underwriter are much the same as for hull claims. Information is needed and obtained from a surveyor and the underwriters claims adjuster will check the detail of the accident against the cover in force as evidenced by the slip/policy. However, liability claims need more information and investigation and the injured parties also need time to access the quantum of their loss. where bodily injury or major property damage has been suffered the appropriate local civil authorities will be carrying out their own investigations and except in very minor affairs underwriters will normally in addition to employing a surveyor retain the services of one of the specialist aviation solicitors or attorneys to act on their behalf having in mind the location of the crash and the likely complexities of the claims.

6.5.1   Establishment of Liability

As with all claims the first need is to establish the facts. It may be literally years before the official reports are published if at all in some countries, so obviously underwriters cannot wait for them but it is important for underwriters to know if their insured is liable.

Next in the case of liability claims it is necessary to establish the liability in accordance with the applicable law. Additional information will be required than that needed purely to settle hull claims as follows:

A copy of the complete passenger list or manifest;
The extent of the bodily injury;
Hospital and doctors reports;
In the event of fatalities, information on ages, income, dependants, next of kin and/or beneficiaries;
Copies of the passenger tickets/flight documentation and the flight plan and the route taken by the aircraft;
The cost and extent of damage to baggage and freight/cargo;
Third party damage caused on the ground with similar additional detail if personal injury or death is involved;
(a copy of the crew manifest will be required but any claims will almost certainly fall under the insured's Employers Liability/Workmens Compensation Act insurance).

Quantum must now be applied to the claims or potential claims in accordance with the law (not forgetting legal fees) so that reserves can be established as follows:

The appropriate conditions of carriage applicable to each passenger as evidenced by the ticket issued to them (It is perfectly possible to have three passengers sat together in an aircraft, each with different conditions of carriage, one who bought his ticket purely for an internal flight with a view to disembarking at a touchdown within the same country; the next to get out at the first landing after leaving the country, in a state which had ratified 'Warsaw' but not 'Hague' and the third, going on to a country that had ratified both Warsaw and Hague. All these three will have different limitations of liability applicable to them).

Underwriters solicitors will need to react to correspondence with the next of kin of those killed and that of their legal representatives and those of the injured; they will need to appoint local lawyers in the country from which deceased originated and to contact and negotiate with these third parties legal representatives.

6.6   PASSENGER LIABILITY
The Insured's legal liability to his passengers is dependent on his relationship to them and the applicable law governing that relationship and falls into two primary categories:

(i)   claims for death, injury, loss, damage or delay arising out of carriage under a contract with the carrier;

(ii)   the same arising out of flights as guests in private aircraft where there is no contract.

Category (i) then sub-divides depending on the passengers contracted journey.

6.6.1 Claims under International Contracts of Carriage:
The nationality of the claimant or the carrier is irrelevant and does not affect the contract of carriage which is determined only by the journey for which the claimant has contracted and for which a ticket has been issued. The Warsaw Convention and the Hague Protocol provide that in respect of carriage for hire or reward or gratuitous carriage by an air transport undertaking a properly completed ticket must be issued and delivered to the passenger before the flight which must contain the place and date of issue, the place of departure and destination, agreed stopping places, name of carrier or carriers and a statement that carriage is subject to the terms of the Warsaw Convention or the Warsaw Convention as amended at the Hague.

If the ticket issued does not comply with all the terms of that Convention the carrier loses those protections of the Convention that limit or exclude his liability though the Convention itself still applies.

In the event of a passenger being killed or injured on board the aircraft or whilst embarking or disembarking and no evidence of negligence or contributory negligence on the part of that passenger can be established, the carrier is liable up to the limits of the Convention unless he has lost the protection of those limits by either a defective ticket as mentioned above or by not issuing a ticket or by wilful misconduct being proved against him.

There is no need for the claimant to prove his case; the operator is liable to the limits of the applicable Convention/Protocol unless he can prove negligence or contributory negligence on the part of the passenger. The claimant has only to establish that his loss at least equals the applicable limits

in the case of Warsaw	125,000 gold francs
in the case of Hague	250,000 gold francs

There are of course exceptions to every rule; the above limits can be breached as already mentioned in the case of a defective ticket or a ticket not issued or by wilful misconduct when, the carrier having lost the benefit of the limits, is liable for whatever loss the claimant can prove (unless he can in turn prove negligence or contributory negligence on the part of the passenger). It will also be remembered that there is provision in the Convention for the carrier and passengers to agree higher limits of liability, and two particular agreements should be borne in mind:

6.6.2 Applicability of Montreal Agreement

As a result of the Montreal Agreement in 1966 air carriers accepted voluntarily to increase their liability where a contract of carriage includes a point of origin, destination or agreed stopping place in the USA to US $75,000 inclusive of costs or US $58,000 exclusive of costs (and agreed to waive Article 20 defences in the Warsaw Convention).

Note − to comply with CAB regulations it is a requirement that the passengers attention must be drawn to the limitations of liability by a notice on a separate piece of paper given to the passenger in his ticket − printed in 10 point type.

6.6.3 The Malta Agreement

The Malta Agreement is an informal understanding between certain European governments to encourage more widespread use of higher Special Contract Limits as a result of which most European airlines contractually offer their passengers higher levels of compensation than those traditionally given by 'Warsaw' or 'Hague' (in the UK it is now a condition for the issue of an Air Transport Licence to a UK operator that he should offer a special contract limit of at least 100,000 SDR's).

Many non-European airlines also have these higher levels.

6.6.4 Insured's Wilful Misconduct

It should be noted that wilful misconduct by the Insured would normally enable the underwriters to avoid liability under their policy; wilful misconduct by his employees, however, normally would not.

The Warsaw Convention and Hague Protocol conditions and limitations apply equally to delay of a passenger as well as to death or bodily injury but for a successful claim for delay it is necessary for the claimant to prove a cause and effect relationship between the delay and the damage.

6.6.5 'Non-International' Contracts of Carriage

These are either domestic, with the journey starting and finishing in the same country with no agreed stopping place outside that country, or between states, one or both of which have not ratified the Warsaw Convention. States which have not ratified the Convention may impose any conditions they so choose particularly in respect of domestic journeys but even those States who have not ratified Warsaw still use Warsaw as a basis of their own law. Whatever the applicable law in these cases a ticket should have been issued and a contract of carriage entered into and the applicable conditions will have to be investigated to establish the carriers liability. It is likely that the liability of the carrier will depend on whether or not he or his employees have been negligent and the local courts will decide the amount of the loss. It may well be that the carrier is a member of IATA and using proper IATA conditions of carriage; this would make him subject to the rules and limitations of 'Warsaw' unless such carriage was not international as defined by 'Warsaw'.

6.6 PRIVATE AIRCRAFT – NO CONTRACT OF CARRIAGE

Most states do not impose any specific duty on operators of aircraft not used for hire or reward and Common law applies. It is usually necessary for such passengers to establish negligence against the operator and to prove the amount of the loss which can be both economic and non economic, such as loss of care and affection etc. to the deceased's dependants. There would be no limitation to the liability of the operator.

6.7 BAGGAGE

Passengers baggage is divided between checked (registered) baggage and unchecked (unregistered) baggage.

Checked baggage is handed over to the carrier, weighed, and a receipt given.

Unchecked baggage consists of the items the passenger personally takes aboard the aircraft, such as brief case, handbag, coat.

6.7.1 Checked (registered) Baggage

The carrier is liable under the Warsaw Convention for loss of or damage to baggage, including damage occasioned by the delay of checked baggage unless he proves that all necessary steps were taken to avoid the loss, or that there was negligence or contributory negligence on the part of the passenger, or that the loss or damage was caused by the negligence of the aircrew.

The carriers liability is limited by the Convention to 250 gold francs per kilogram but is unlimited if it is established that he failed to issue a properly completed baggage check (normally now built into the passenger ticket itself) or there was wilful misconduct on his part.

When a passenger buys a ticket he is normally given a 'free' baggage weight allowance dependant on the airline and 'class' in which he is travelling; therefore, in the event of a claim his maximum indemnity is readily perceivable unless he paid for excess baggage or if he had declared the value of his baggage and paid an additional fee accordingly, both of which exceptions would be of course recorded by the airline. Where a declaration of value has been made and the fee paid the carriers maximum liability becomes that of the declared value.

The Warsaw Convention includes a provision for liability arising from delay; the interpretation of this provision is open to debate particularly in that the maximum potential recoveries hardly justify major law suits giving establishment to precedent. However, the airlines, for public relations reasons if no other, normally look reasonably on claims for the purchase of essential clothes, toiletries etc. for use until such time as the mislaid baggage is recovered.

6.7.2 Unchecked Baggage

Because it is in the possession of the passenger himself it is encumbent on him to exercise due care. To establish a claim against the carrier it is normally necessary for the passenger to prove negligence by the carrier. If a claim is established the Convention limits the carriers liability to 5,000 gold francs.

The big airlines are frequently self insured for the baggage risks and have their own baggage claims departments. Both these departments, and underwriters if they are covering the risk, will look for the passenger to abide by time limits given by the Convention regarding notice of loss, damage or delay of the baggage. It will be appreciated that there does not have to be an accident to the aircraft for baggage to be damaged or lost; in fact the main causes of claims are mishandling, pilferage and delivery to the wrong destination.

Baggage claims arising from non-international carriage or private flights, or the issue of an incorrect ticket are dealt with in the same way as passenger claims in similar circumstances.

6.8   GOODS/FREIGHT/CARGO

Goods are shipped under an Airwaybill (AWB) or Air Consignment Note which is deemed to be the contract of carriage. on international carriage, as defined by Warsaw, the Convention applies and the carrier is liable for loss or damage, including damage occasioned by delay to goods shipped by air; unless he can prove

(a)   that all necessary steps to avoid the loss were taken;

(b)   that there was contributory negligence by the consignor;

(c)   that there has been contributory negligence on the part of the aircrew;

the carriers liability is limited to 250 gold francs per kilo unless a higher limit has been declared to and agreed by the carrier. The carrier cannot limit his liability if

−   a properly completed Airwaybill was not issued;

−   there was wilful misconduct on the part of the carrier or his employees.

It will be understood that one of the most important facts to establish is the weight of the goods lost; the Airwaybill has to state the number of pieces shipped as well as the weight of the goods. (Note − although the weight to be taken into consideration in the event of a claim is that of the pieces of the overall shipment that have actually been lost or delayed, nevertheless if their damage or delay affects the value of the total shipment then the weight of the total shipment must be taken into account).

6.8.1 Carriers Responsibility

The carriers responsibility (in accordance with Article 18 of 'Warsaw') comprises the period when the goods are in his charge whether in an aerodrome or on board an aircraft or in the case of a landing outside an aerodrome in any place whatsoever.

Most carriers make special arrangements for the carriage of currency, diamonds, gold and other valuables, and in the event of a loss checks must be made to ensure all security procedures were followed. Their comparatively small weight and consequently the carriers low limit of liability on such items compared to their high value means that it is critical that all documentation is correctly completed or the carriers liability, becoming unlimited thereby, could be exceedingly high and possibly beyond his policy limits.

6.8.2 Dangerous Goods

Explosives, poisons, radioactive material and other dangerous articles shipped by air must be done so in accordance with IATA regulations specifying, inter alia, packaging, marking and maximum quantities per aircraft, these regulations must be strictly complied with.

The carrier has a liability under 'Warsaw' for delay of goods carried with identical limits and rules for those applicable to baggage. Consequential loss arising out of delay (e.g. loss of market) is not covered by insurers.

6.9 PRODUCTS LIABILITY/AIRPORT OWNERS AND OPERATORS LIABILITY

On receipt of notice of a claim the adjuster must, as always, obtain the maximum amount of information, and consider that information in the light of the wording of the policy issued. Assuming that the facts of the case are not blatantly in breach of the policy conditions and that there is prima facie a claim under that policy, then unless it is a minor matter that can be settled by simple negotiation, the adjusters will appoint a lawyer and together they will negotiate the processes of the law until final settlement of the claim.

6.10 CLAIMS HANDLING – GENERAL

6.10.1 Notification

No action will be taken on a claim unless and until the insured advises the underwriters, usually via his brokers. The insured is required by the conditions of his policy to give immediate notice of any event likely to give rise to a claim. He must furnish full particulars, give notice of impending prosecution, render further information and assistance as required and not act in any way to the detriment or prejudice of underwriters.

He must not make any admission of liability or payment or offer or promise of payment without the written consent of underwriters. Any letters or communications he receives from third parties must be passed to underwriters unanswered.

The insured could well invalidate his policy if he does not give timely advice.

6.10.2 Validity

The insured can only claim if he has a valid policy covering the loss and an insurable interest therein. The policy can be one of indemnity only and the insured may not make a profit (Agreed values are not deemed to be in contradiction of this principle as the law considers that the measure of indemnity is simply agreed at the beginning of each period of insurance rather than waiting until the time of the loss).

6.10.3 Non-Contribution

The insureds policy will almost certainly contain a **Non-Contribution** clause whereby the policy shall not apply to claims which are payable under any other policy except in respect of any excess beyond the amount which would be payable under such policy.

If the insured were able to collect the same claim under different policies the principle of indemnity would be breached as his total recovery would exceed his loss – this is consequently precluded.

If it transpires that the insured does have other policies the loss will be divided equitably between them.

If those other policies also contain a non-contribution clause the situation could arise whereby they all cancel each other and the insured would be left without cover. Since this position would be absurd in practice each policy would pay its rateable proportion of the loss giving equal distribution of that loss between the several insurers.

6.10.4 **Policy Limits**
Whatever the insured's liability, underwriters will only protect him against third party claims up to the policy limits preselected by him and for which premium has been paid. Whilst underwriters will (normally) in addition to the limit of liability defray legal costs and expenses incurred with their consent they will limit the amount they pay for such cost and expenses to such proportion of them as the policy limit of indemnity bears to the amount paid for compensatory damages.

6.10.5 **Policy Interpretation**
The interpretation of contract (policy) wording can only be decided by the courts. Once the meaning of a phrase or word has been decided by them all future uses of that phrase or word will be deemed to have the same meaning except where the context in which they are set clearly shows otherwise. Where there is no such precedent the court will consider first the whole of the policy so that the word(s) in dispute are not taken out of context and will look to give the same interpretation to them each time they appear unless it is clear that a different meaning is intended.

They will always give greater weight and precedence to written words over printed words. They will always apply the normal rules of grammar and, unless impossible to do so, construe the words in their ordinary every day meaning. They will seek to broadly construe the policy to express the total meaning of the parties involved. Since it will have been underwriters who prepared the wording any doubt or ambiguity will be construed against them and in favour of the insured (Contra Proferentem rule).

6.10.6 **Arbitration**
Policies normally contain an Arbitration clause to enable any reasonable dispute or difference between the underwriters and the insured to be arbitrated in accordance with the appropriate statutory provisions rather than submit them both to the delay and expense of the courts.

6.10.7 **Repudiation of Liability**
Underwriters can repudiate liability under the policy if there has been a breach of warranty, non-disclosure or misrepresentation by the insured. If the underwriters elect not to do so such conditions are waived.

Note — Most US and Canadian policies have a clause imposing a duty on underwriters to defend the insured against claims made against them, however remote. The courts in the US have upheld the view that the insured is entitled to a defence even when he is in dispute with his insurers who believe a policy condition has been breached or an exclusion clause operates.

6.11 **SETTLEMENT OF LIABILITY CLAIMS**
Having determined that they will indemnify the insured and having assumed their option to take absolute control of all negotiations, it will be underwriters decision as to how they will make the actual settlement with the Third Party, that is to settle out of court or go to trial.

6.11.1 **Out of Court Settlements**
It may be in the insureds interest to settle out of court to prevent adverse publicity; on the other hand this may well not be in the underwriters own interest which is to settle as cheaply and equitably as possible.

In fact settlement out of court will always be attempted particularly where the insured is clearly liable and the question of quantum of damages is the only issue. It may also be attempted where liability is doubtful and compromise is sought. Out of court settlements save the long delay of waiting for the trial to commence which itself could take weeks. It also saves the considerable expenses involved, win or lose.

Even where they are not liable under a policy, underwriters may decide that it is in their own best interests to settle comparatively minor sums in order to save the huge expense of a trial at the end of which they stand little or no chance of recovering costs.

In fact after a major loss underwriters usually provide their lawyers with a pool of money from which those lawyers can negotiate where possible immediate settlement, within the law and in return for releases, to save both delay and litigation expenses.

6.11.2 **Court Settlement**
Before finally determining to go to trial underwriters need to consider the applicable laws under which the trial will take place. Aviation is international and the plaintiff can be the resident of any country and the applicable law may be that of anywhere in the world. The underwriters, having assumed the insured's liability, will have to do so wherever the case may be legitimately brought. Private International Law is the branch of English law which deals in cases in which some relevant fact has a geographical connection with a foreign country. In England it revolves round the following basic questions:

(a) have the English courts jurisdiction to deal with the specific issue?

(b) under what law should the issue be decided? (English courts can apply foreign law where so required).

(c) on what basis shall the English courts decide whether or not the judgement of a foreign court should be recognised and enforced in England?

Most other countries have similar provisions in their judicial systems and in the USA one State can apply and try a case under the laws of another State. So it will be seen that even if the litigation takes place in underwriters own country the laws of another country could be applied.

6.11.3 **Keeping Records**
The claims adjuster and the broker should remember and the client should be warned that courts are entitled to see, and litigants entitled to demand, production of any document which is in their view relevant to the case in hand. So no insurers report other than one prepared specifically for the purposes of litigation can be privileged from production; therefore when preparing records and making notes on a file they should be made with the knowledge that they may have to be justified in court at a later date.

6.11.4 **Structured Settlement**
Assuming both the principle of payment of a claim and quantum to have been agreed it is possible for the actual payment to be made as a Structured Settlement

as opposed to a flat 'in full' cash sum. A structured settlement makes use of one or more annuities bought at the time of settlement from a life insurance company but so structured as to give periodic payments; this can be extremely advantageous to a child orphaned by a crash, and could give guaranteed income for life or could in certain circumstances have tax benefits to the recipient. There is also usually a discount in this form of settlement in underwriters favour.

6.11.5 Special Settlements
As previously mentioned, payment of a claim once agreed should proceed with speed; the market's reputation is at stake and delay can be costing the insured money. It is the brokers task to collect the proportions due from the individual underwriters of the risk.

Those due from the individual Lloyd's Underwriters are collected in bulk from the Lloyd's Policy Signing Office either by means of a Special Settlement, a system by which the broker receives funds on the third working day after submitting the claim and prepared documentation to the Signing Office, or if the claim is not of a size to warrant a Special Settlement then as part of the normal settlement of funds between the broker and Lloyd's which takes place the Friday of the week following processing by the Signing office (so a maximum of 10 working days and a minimum of five working days).

The proportions due from members of the Institute of London Underwriters (ILU) are collected in bulk in a like manner to those from Lloyd's with the same two alternative routes to collection.

Where companies are not members of the ILU the broker deals directly with them and settlement is made to the broker by cheque (or if they are overseas by telegraphic transfer) to preferably coincide with receipt of the funds coming in from the two bureaux.

As the funds are accumulated the broker remits them to the loss payee in the speediest practical manner.

6.12   ON COMPLETION OF SETTLEMENT (HULL AND LIABILITY)

6.12.1 Proximate Cause
The adjuster will need to consider again the proximate cause, that is 'the active, efficient cause that sets in motion the train of events which brings about a result without the intervention of any other force started and working actively from a new and independent source', i.e. the real cause of the accident. (Remember there would not have been a payment in the first place if the proximate cause had been an excluded peril under the policy).

6.12.2 Subrogation
Under the terms of the policy the underwriter is subrogated to the rights and remedies of the insured and can 'stand in his place'. So indemnity having been given and payment made the underwriter may be able to extinguish or diminish his own loss by subrogation which is the Common Law right to recover the monies paid out from the Third Party who is actually responsible for the loss. For example, the manufacturer of the whole or part of the aircraft.

6.12.3 Records and IBNR's (Incurred but not Reported Claims)

Underwriters will expect the adjuster to keep careful records of claims paid and outstanding including a split of those claims into category (Hull or Liability and what type of Liability), type (Fixed Wing, Helicopter, Micro-light etc.) and use (Private, Commercial, Industrial Aid etc.) and to develop a system based on those records of assessing claims that might have been incurred but not reported (IBNR's).

6.13 CLAIMS HANDLING ON REINSURANCE CONTRACTS

Unless stated to the contrary the original direct underwriter negotiates claims not only on his own behalf but on that of his reinsurers as well, settlement being in accordance with a full reinsurance clause such as, for example, clause NMA 416 below.

REINSURANCE WARRANTY CLAUSE (FULL R/I.Clause No.1)

Being a Reinsurance of and warranted same gross rate, terms and conditions as and to follow the settlements of the ....
....Company and that said Company retains during the currency of this policy at least ....
on the identical subject matter and risk and in identically the same proportion on each separate part thereof, but in the event of the retained line being less than as above, Underwriters' lines to be proportionately reduced.

3/6/43

N.M.A.416

Alternatively the reinsurance might be placed with either a claims cooperation clause such as AV 21 whereby the negotiation and settlement of claims is left in the hands of the reinsured underwriter, subject to him giving advice to his reinsurers within a specific period of any loss or losses which may fall under the reinsurance and cooperating with them in the adjustment and settlement thereof. This Clause might for example be used on large risks where the original underwriter has inadequate experience.

CLAIMS COOPERATION CLAUSE

Notwithstanding anything herein contained to the contrary, it is a condition precedent to any liability under this policy that

(a)   the Reassured shall upon knowledge of any loss or losses which may give rise to a claim under this policy advise the Underwriters thereof within seven days,

(b)   the Reassured shall furnish the Underwriters with all information available respecting such loss or losses and shall co-operate with the Underwriters in the adjustment and settlement thereof.

5/5/58

Aviation 21

Or with a Claims Control Clause such as AV 25 where it is the reinsurer who takes control of all negotiations and settlements acting both on his own part and that of the reinsured underwriter. This Clause would be used where the reinsured has inadequate experience and/or particularly where the reinsured's own retention of risk is not considered sufficient.

CLAIMS CONTROL CLAUSE

Notwithstanding anything herein contained to the contrary, it is a condition precedent to any liability under this policy that

(a)   the Reassured shall, upon knowledge of any loss or losses which may give rise to a claim under this policy, advise the Underwriters thereof by cable within 72 hours;

(b)   the Reassured shall furnish the Underwriters with all information available respecting such loss or losses, and the Underwriters shall have the right to appoint adjusters, assessors and/or surveyors and to control all negotiations, adjustments and settlements in connection with such loss or losses.

3/6/58

Aviation 25

In cases where the reinsurers consider that the reinsured's experience is inadequate and/or his retention of risk is insufficient it is likely that the reinsurers will wish to retain control not just of the Claims settlements but the rating of the risk as well in which case they will require Clause AV 41, Reinsurance Underwriting and Claims Control Clause; in fact the most commonly used.

REINSURANCE UNDERWRITING & CLAIMS CONTROL CLAUSE

1.   being a Reinsurance of the.................. Company and, except as provided by paragraph 2 hereof, warranted the same gross rate, terms and conditions as the said Company as agreed at inception, and that the said Company retains during the currency of this policy at least............ on the identical subject matter and risk and in identically the same proportion on each separate part thereof, but in the event of the retained line being less than as above, Underwriters' lines to be proportionately reduced.

2.   Subject to the foregoing, it is a condition precedent to any liability under this Reinsurance that:

(a)   no amendment to the terms or conditions or additions to or deletions from the original policy shall be binding upon Underwriters hereon unless prior agreement has been obtained from the said Underwriters;

(b)   the Reassured shall upon knowledge of any loss or losses which may give rise to a claim under this policy, advise the Underwriters by cable within 72 hours;

(c)   the Reassured shall furnish the Underwriters with all information available respecting such loss or losses, and the Underwriters shall have the sole right to appoint adjusters, assessors, surveyors and/or lawyers and to control all negotiations, adjustments and settlements in connection with such loss or losses.

9/6/65

Aviation 41

6.14 LETTERS OF CREDIT (LOC'S)

The use of Letters of Credit in a purely insurance context became fairly wide – spread from 1962 onwards, first as a substitute for cash advances and more recently for unearned premium reserves required by the American ceding market.

A Letter of Credit creates an irrevocable undertaking by the issuing bank in favour of the beneficiary that payment will be made provided the beneficiary complies with the terms of the Letter of Credit and consequently is normally accepted by the US regulatory authorities in support of assets (or as a deduction from loss reserves for reinsurance recoverable) in the books of a US Ceding Company

Special Features: –

(a) DRAWINGS – Drawings under Letters of Credit are normally made by draft on the issuing bank.

(b) AMENDMENTS – Amendments to the face value of Letters of Credit may take place with the Account Party and issuing bank's agreement in the case of increases, and the agreement of the Account Party, bank and beneficiary in the case of decreases.

(c) CANCELLATION – Once issued Letters of Credit cannot be cancelled except with the written agreement of the opener (otherwise known as the 'Account Party') and the beneficiary.

LOC's are normally issued for periods of not less than one year, and must contain an "evergreen clause" which automatically extends the validity of the letter of credit unless the issuing bank has given the beneficiary not less than 30 days due notice of non-renewal.

It is recommended that brokers endeavour to secure 3 year Letters of Credit and extend them at 24 months thus obtaining early warning of any reinsurer who intends to cancel.

TABLE OF STATUTES/LEGISLATION/CONVENTIONS AND TREATIES

Montreal Protocol 1978, 2.5.2.
Multimodal Transport Convention (Geneva 1980), 2.13.

Pan American Convention 1928, 1.2.
Protection of Aircraft Act 1973, 2.11.

Rome Convention 1933, 2.5.
Rome Convention 1952, 2.5,1.

Tokyo Convention 1963, 2.10.
Tokyo Convention Act 1967, 2.10.5.
Two Freedoms Agreement 1944, 2.7.

Unfair Contract Terms Act 1977, 2.14.1.
UK Rules of the Air and Air Traffic Control Regulations 1985, 4.5.

Warsaw Convention 1929, 1.

TABLE OF CASES

Re AIR DISASTER IN LOCKERBIE, SCOTLAND, ON DECEMBER 21 1988
It was ruled by Judge Platt, US District Court, New York Eastern District (1990) that Punitive Damages not recoverable under Warsaw Convention

"While need to encourage the airline industry's growth may now be obsolete, it is only the political branches which have the power to repudiate or amend the Warsaw Convention ... In its most recent ruling on the Warsaw Convention, the Supreme Court once again admonished the courts that "to alter, amend, or add to any treaty would be... an exercise of political functions" ... Therefore, in interpreting the Warsaw Convention in the only manner consistent with the shared expectations of the contracting parties at the time, this Court is compelled to hold that the Warsaw Convention bars plaintiff's punitive damage claims whether or not wilful misconduct exists."   (5.4.)

CHAN v KOREAN AIRLINES
(1985 – affirmed 1987 – reaffirmed Supreme Court 1989) – arising out of Korean air disaster 1983 (shoot down in Sea of Japan) – American Courts attitude to limiting liability set by international treaty.   (2.3.1.)

COROCRAFT v PAN AMERICAN WORLD AIRWAYS (1969)
Consignment notes must show weight but other detail required by Warsaw may be omitted if neither useful nor necessary.   (1.5.3.)

EGAM v KOLLSMAN INSTRUMENT CORP. (1967).
Print size on tickets referring to the limitation of the carrier's liability must be of a size and location so as to be easily readable (1.5.1.) Plus use of other means of transport between two flights does not affect the position of the air carrier provided such use naturally forms part of the whole journey   (1.5.6.)

FOTHERGILL v MONARCH AIRLINES (House of Lords 1981).
A case started in 1978 and turning on the interpretation of the word 'damage' use in the phrase 'liable for damage' in article 18(1) of Warsaw   (1.4,)

GREIN v IMPERIAL AIRWAYS (1937)
Consideration whether a carriage was international or not. (Unamended Convention) Green L.J.:

"The rules are rules relating not to journeys, not to flights, not to parts of journeys, but to carriage performed under one .... contract of carriage. The contract .... is, so to speak, the unit to which attention is to be paid in considering whether the carriage to be performed under it is international or not."   (1.5.1.)

Re HIJACKING OF PAN AMERICAN WORLD AIRWAYS INC. AIRCRAFT
At Karachi International Airport Pakistan on September 5 1986 (F supp 17 Southern District, New York – 1990).

Judge Sprizzo "punitive damages are a part of Common Law tort remedies ... and no language in the Convention preempts or precludes such claims."

(5.4.)

LISA v ALITALIA (1966)
Print size on tickets referring to the limitation of the carriers liability must be of a size and location so as to be easily readable. (1.5.1.)

MARTENS v FLYING TIGER LINE (1965)
Carrier must deliver the passenger a ticket a sufficient time before the flight to enable the passenger to make other arrangements if the conditions contained do not suit. (1.5.1.)

NORTHWESTERN CASUALTY CO. v McNULTY (1962)
Federal Appeal Court, Florida — Motor case. Court ruled it would not permit an insurer to be held liable for Punitive Damages imposed as a deterrent or punishment on the insured driver. (5.4.4.)

WARREN v FLYING TIGER LINE (1965)
Carrier must deliver the passenger a ticket a sufficient time before the flight to enable the passenger to make other arrangements if the conditions contained do not suit. (1.5.1.)

68